Living the Presence
of the Spirit

Jack Haberer

GENEVA

Geneva Press
Louisville, Kentucky

To Barbie,

who has taught me what it is to live
in the presence of unconditional love.

© 2001 John H. Haberer Jr.

All rights reserved.
No part of this book may be reproduced or
transmitted in any form or by any means, electronic or mechanical,
including photocopying, recording, or by any information storage or
retrieval system, without permission in writing from the publisher.
For information, address Geneva Press,
100 Witherspoon Street, Louisville, Kentucky 40202-1396.

Book design by Sharon Adams
Cover design by Pam Poll

First edition
Published by Geneva Press
Louisville, Kentucky

This book is printed on acid-free paper that meets the
American National Standards Institute Z39.48 standard.♾

PRINTED IN THE UNITED STATES OF AMERICA

01 02 03 04 05 06 07 08 09 10 — 10 9 8 7 6 5 4 3 2 1

Library of Congress Cataloging-in-Publication Data

A catalog record for this book is available from the Library of Congress.

ISBN 0-664-50180-X

Contents

Foreword

*I*t makes me nervous to say it. I don't want you to misunderstand me. But you need to read this book. Doing so will help you understand much better the person and presence of the Holy Spirit. Leaders of spirituality are careful to preserve the element of mystery when speaking of the Spirit. Jesus observes that the Spirit, like the wind, "blows where it chooses, and you hear the sound of it, but you do not know where it comes from or where it goes." To think you can better understand the Spirit is almost sacrilege.

In a time when books on spirituality are proliferating, we need to reground the experience of God in the Word. Many writers draw heavily from the insights of medieval mystics and eastern mysticism, from Catholic monasteries and Pentecostal revivals, and make only token reference to a few favorite verses from scripture.

This book stands apart. Instead of accumulating personal experiences and curious speculations, it grounds the experience of God in the Word. Scripture provides the content, and Jesus provides the center of the drama. Jack Haberer does not deny the ultimate mystery of the Spirit, but he does make clear truths taught in scripture regarding the person of the Holy Spirit and about living a life filled with the Spirit. Most notably, the author asserts that the Spirit is given once, never to be withdrawn, regardless of how elusive the perception of the Spirit may be. I find his arguments compelling.

The proliferation of books on spirituality hints of its growth in popularity as both an experience and a discipline. *Living the Presence* can help the movement surge by grounding it in scripture, by rooting the experiential elements within a solid, grace-filled theological framework, and by inciting thinking believers to catch the fire of the Spirit.

The author tells the Spirit's story through an intriguing biographical format. Posed as the protagonist driving the biblical drama, the Presence is introduced in the creative process, communes in the garden, is squandered in humanity's sin, makes numerous visitations upon God's people, overshadows the incarnate Christ and ultimately indwells the redeemed people of God. Every step along the way of the story provides a valuable key to help us live in the Presence.

In spite of its profundity this book is an easy read, bringing Bible stories alive better than most animated films. It will come alive for you, too. As his doctoral advisor, trust me when I say that Jack's dissertation was not such an easy read. Valuable for your purposes, this book is undergirded by exhaustive research. Jack knows his subject matter.

After you read this text, invite your Bible study class to make it the heart of their next study series. Chances are good that they too will echo the words, "It's so biblical and it makes so much sense. How come I've never heard this before?"

Ben Campbell Johnson
Professor Christian Spirituality, Emeritus
Columbia Theological Seminary

Preface

At Elim Bible Institute, Maundy Thursday was an odd time to be having a religious experience. Sure this was one of the holiest days of the church calendar. But as we students hurried to find our seats for chapel service, we had only one thing on our minds. Spring break. Immediately following the benediction, we'd be liberated from the wintry snow to bask in warmer places to the south. In fact, the irreverent buzz among us students brought a curt scolding from the school's vice president at the beginning of the service.

The chatter was displaced by an embarrassed hush.

The organ began to play. We stood and opened our hymnals and began to sing, "At the cross, at the cross where I first saw the light . . ." All four verses. Then another favorite, "On a hill far away stood an old rugged cross, the emblem of suff'ring and shame . . ." Again all four verses. Then we segued right into another, "When I survey the wondrous cross on which the Prince of glory died, my richest gain I count but loss and pour contempt on all my pride."

As we began the second stanza, an obscure scripture verse crossed my mind, "The veil of the temple was rent in twain from top to bottom." I had heard the verse before but had never given it any thought. But in a moment's time, my mind's eye saw something I'd never seen before. As if waking up on a bus after traveling all night and discovering a panorama totally unimagined, I saw the whole Bible story as I'd never seen it before.

Like one of those moments when your life passes before you, the tumultuous romance between God and humanity raced through my mind in rapid-fire images. In the unfolding of a story, I relived the rending of affection between the first couple and their Creator. I watched the covenant making between the Lord and an elderly pregnant Sarah and Abraham. I heard the thundering tumult of Yahweh's mountainous encounter with Moses. I listened with Elijah to hear the voice of God amid the sheer silence. I thrilled to visit the humble Bethlehem child. I shuddered over the horror at Golgotha, and I watched as the veil was "rent in twain from top to bottom." Then I reached sensory overload—overwhelming joy—as the gift of the Spirit rained down.

In the process, I felt God's love as I had never felt it before. I sensed that I had become a dwelling for God, purchased at an incredible price by the Savior.

I sobbed.

Then came the final verse: "Were the whole realm of nature mine, that were a present far too small. Love so amazing, so divine, demands my soul, my life, my all."

My life was perceptibly changed. My perspective on the Christian life would never be the same. In the months and years that followed, in both undergraduate and graduate studies, I spent countless hours digging through the scriptures to search out the details of my Maundy Thursday insights. I took special courses just to do further research. Strangely, I often caught my eyes tearing while typing the final draft of papers. In fact—oh-oh . . . here I go again.

To my gleeful surprise, professors responded repeatedly, "Good insights. You're on to something here. Stick with it."

All the while, I grew personally and developed a pastoral ministry that provided a fertile testing ground for these thoughts. Every so often a member would exclaim, "I get it. Now I know what you're talking about!" Then again, gracious, supportive congregations have continually pressed me to refine my teaching in ways that not only brought them emotionally glistening "aha's" but also could prove practical for their everyday lives.

Strikingly, every time I have preached on the theme or taught a seminar on it—whether at my own church or at a conference—

someone has commented, "What you said makes so much sense. And it's so obviously biblical. How come I've never heard it before?"

These insights seem to hold a key to living with God that has been overlooked for centuries. Yet, who am I to be making such a grandiose claim?

For years, a healthy ounce of skepticism held me in check. "There's nothing new under the sun," says Ecclesiastes. I feared that there must be some major flaw in my thinking. Sure, I had found a coherent study in scripture itself. But after years of research, I had yet to find even a single book or article written to support my approach. I must have made a glaring mistake somewhere, or fallen victim to a horrendous false assumption—or maybe I'm just off-my-rocker. I wondered.

When I heard that an extension program for doctor of ministry studies would be available nearby, I questioned the seminary representative: "Do the students get to write dissertations?"

"Well, yes. But don't worry. In the D.Min. program, you're really expected to do a practical project that you write up. It's a lot less work than the kind of academic research a Ph.D. demands."

"But if I want to do a serious dissertation, with lots of research, will I be allowed?"

He looked at me like I were an Army general volunteering for KP duty. He spoke haltingly, "Well, uh, if you'd like to do a full-blown dissertation, with, uh, lots of research, uh, why um, there's nothing wrong with that. We'd be happy to have you do that."

And so I did. I entered the seminary, attended the classes, and dug into the research. To my surprise, I fell upon the work of Samuel Terrien, particularly his *The Elusive Presence.*[1] I bought six copies. No, I didn't need six copies. I just had to have them. In his book, Terrien explored thoughts similar to mine, particularly those relating to the Old Testament. He also provided a level of scholarly research I could never hope to do on my own.

---

1. Samuel Terrien, *The Elusive Presence: Toward a New Biblical Theology* (San Francisco: Harper & Row, 1978).

Although his handling of the New Testament took a direction different from mine—for which I eventually took him to task in my dissertation—his Old Testament work was formidable. It both strengthened and enlarged my claim that the presence of Holy Spirit is the driving theme of scripture.

The research, which set me to reading literally hundreds of sources, provided many refinements to my ideas.[2] But the central idea never changed. In fact, it became clearer and clearer.

That idea is what this book is about. My reason for writing about it is, simply, that I have an unquenchable desire to share with others the life-changing perspective it has given me.

Yes, at Elim Bible Institute, Maundy Thursday was an odd time for such an insight. But God timed it perfectly. I hope that today proves to be God's timing for you. Indeed, I pray that you may find your imagination quickened and your heart expanded to overflowing as mine has been.

May you too discover the wonder of living the presence of the Holy Spirit.

---

2. If you want footnotes and references, the dissertation that inspired this book is on file at Columbia Theological Seminary in Decatur, Georgia, under the title "The Presence of the Spirit: Elusive or Abiding? Toward a Theology of Spirituality," by John H. Haberer Jr., 1989.

Acknowledgments

A book that has taken over twenty-five years to develop could not have been born were it not for the help of many midwives. As an avid student both of biblical revelation and of others' acquired wisdom, I acknowledge that the ideas contained in this manuscript are largely the integration of insights gleaned from many other greater minds and deeper faiths. In fact, any lasting impact these thoughts might have on you in all likelihood will have come from one of them. I cannot proceed without extending the thanks each one is due.

The early years of discovering the person and work of Holy Spirit came at Elim Bible Institute, where then-vice-president David Edwards repeatedly pressed me to think through the faith experience I was so passionately feeling. Paul Johansson, the dean of students (now president), did not let me settle for a theoretical knowledge of God; it must get down into the guts of living and into the will of our choosing.

At Roberts Wesleyan College, theology professor Stan Magill and philosophy professor Michael Petersen pressed not only theological-intellectual acuity; they expanded my world into one where all truth is God's truth, no matter where it may be found. At Gordon-Conwell Theological Seminary, Gordon Fee brought scholarly study of Holy Spirit to a level I had never conceived of, and Richard Lovelace introduced me to the *novel* idea that the Spirit's footsteps can be tracked within mainline Protestant churches. At Columbia Theological Seminary, Walter Brueggemann introduced me to the work of Samuel Terrien—which reassured me that these ideas were not totally off the wall—and Ben Johnson coached me through a dissertation that corrected and sharpened so many points of integration between scripture, church, and personal spiritual formation. Thanks goes also to several other scholars who provided thorough and thoughtful feedback on the dissertation, namely, Sam Terrien, Arthur Baird, David Willis-Watkins, and David Buttrick.

The formulation and articulation of these ideas have all been tested on the unsuspecting congregations of Trinity Presbyterian Church in Satellite Beach, Florida, and Clear Lake Presbyterian Church in Houston, Texas. In those years at Trinity, a very forgiving congregation put up with my preoccupation with the doctoral studies—even while building a new sanctuary—and affirmed so many teachings and sermons related to the Presence. Many of those presentations were so theoretical and obtuse! How gracious that congregation was to persevere through those teachings and to teach me how to teach others. Then again, from time to time, one member or another would report an "aha" experience, a quiet epiphany, by saying, "Now I get it!" Those responses would send chills down my spine, encouraging me to keep pounding away from every angle till they all got it.

One who not only had the "aha" but kept adding, "When are you going to write the book?" was Becky Cavallucci. As a dollar-a-year church administrator (inflation has pushed her salary up to about $1.31 per year), she gave countless hours of service to support our ministry there. All the more, she proofread the dissertation, the cruelest and most unusual punishment known to humanity; she attended every teaching session I ever presented; and she kept pressing me to get the word out. Linda Howard, my secretary-editor-extraordinaire, matched Becky word for word in the proofreading, thereby turning the dissertation into something that at least had good grammar. Friends Hartley and Brenda Caldwell, Ruth and Doug Paauwe, Scott and Tricia Jordan, Bud and Ethel Earhart, Joyce and Ron Daley, and Audrey and Jim Garnett all coaxed the best out of me along the way.

At Clear Lake Presbyterian, my associate pastor, Barbara Carmichael, not only read the manuscript; she offered serious critique and pressed for some helpful improvements. Jeff and

Janet Williams pushed me frequently to get off the dime to publish the work. My prayer partners, Byder Wilde, Judy Franklin, Sharon Jenkins, Sarah Korkowski, MaryAnn Stickney, Carl Bookout, and Cliff Poe all prayed the book into existence. Jimmy and Marilu McGregor provided support of every kind. And Barb Robertson, my executive assistant and veteran editor of *Texas Fisherman Magazine,* edited the manuscript, introducing many of the creative turns of phrase. You'll be glad to know that I did resist adding suggested analogies from the mating habits of flounder and sea bass.

In the meantime, it was the enthusiastic response of my first senior pastor, George Callahan, that finally did get me off the dime to push for publication, and Tom Long's vision and help at Geneva Press helped turn the proverbial sow's ear into what I hope you will find to be a silk purse. Then again, encouragement, fresh ideas, and extra prodding have come over the years from such friends and colleagues as Rosalie Potter, Bruce Larson, Elmer Floyd, Scott Leslie, Malcolm Smith, and Bob Steele. The support of family, namely Mom, Tobi and Steve, Beth and Norman, Geoff and Peggy, Dad and Ann, and the whole Hutchens-Niswander-Clark clan, has coaxed out the best from me.

Over the past quarter century, the help of so many others has been crowded out of memory to this scatterbrain. To those who have not been mentioned, please accept not only my thanks but also my apology for the oversight. May the God whom you have served humbly reward you gloriously.

Three contributors to this effort cannot be overlooked, for they have endured the hardships of ministry that are particularly unique to the life of a pastor's family. My understanding and experience of Holy Spirit has grown in tandem with the personal lessons I have been taught by David and Kelly, who today are two of the finest young Christian adults a father could hope to have as friends. Most of all, one other friend, my beloved partner these past twenty-five years, possesses a depth of Spirit-infused character that deserves expression of thanks that exceed the power of words to say them. In her presence I have come to know a love like no other. It is to Barbie that this book is dedicated.

The Rest of the Story

*T*he crucifixion of Christ didn't get the job done. That's not to say that the cross does not stand at the crux of history. It's just to say that after Jesus' crucifixion, his disciples returned to fishing. The Jesus Movement ended. Life went on as before.

The resurrection of Christ didn't get the job done. That's not to say that Jesus' resurrection from the dead did not defeat life's greatest enemy. It's just to say that after his resurrection, his disciples went into hiding. The Jesus Movement went underground. His followers cowered under the cloak of fear.

The crucifixion and resurrection of Christ didn't get the job done. The world's reconciliation with God, made possible by the cross, and humanity's victory over death, made possible by the resurrection, would have come to naught were it not for the little-recognized rest of the story.

We need to know the rest of the story.

For years, Paul Harvey has been reporting "The Rest of the Story." His daily broadcasts under that title have held radio listeners spellbound as he has recited the stories of famous people and historic events, spicing them with little-known facts, surprising backgrounds, and overlooked results. Given the new angles presented, the familiar stories have taken on new meaning.

When it comes to telling the gospel, Christians have been hearing only part of the story. Christ's cross and resurrection stand incomplete. Left by themselves, those two events carry no lasting impact.

The church has built itself around the cross. Literally speaking, the cross hangs at the visual center of most church sanctuaries. Purposefully speaking, the cross focuses the church's preaching: "We preach Christ and him crucified." Rightly has many a preacher exclaimed the centrality of the cross. Indeed, by suffering that ignominious death, Jesus was carrying the sins of the world, making way for God's forgiveness to be embraced by whosoever repents and believes. He also was re-creating humanity, this time based upon the call to all to take up their crosses, deny themselves, and follow him.

However, every preacher has also known that a dead Savior cannot save the world. The message of the cross is incomplete without the message of the resurrection.

When it comes to telling the gospel, the church calendar revolves around its celebration of the resurrection. Note the attendance on Easter Sunday! In fact, the Christian calendar gets set by establishing the traditional date for Easter each year, and then adding or subtracting Sundays from there. Morcover, the early church was so conscious of its resurrection beginnings that it changed the Sabbath observance from Saturday to Sunday. The church called it the Lord's Day. The resurrection brings not only the ultimate promise of spending eternity with God; it also brings the eternal power of God into believers' lives here and now.

However, when you look back at the band of followers that met the resurrected Christ, their experience of almighty power is hardly overwhelming. Instead you find a group of insecure, bewildered sheep in search of a shepherd.

To understand how these "fumblebums" were transformed into the most dynamic force for change in the first century—as was said of them, "They have turned the world upside down"— you need to know the rest of the story.

The rest of the story is seldom told and even less understood. The holiday that marks it is passed over like any Sunday in "Ordinary Time." The neglect of the story led one Presbyterian pastor to title a sermon provocatively, "Father, Son, and What's-Its-Name."

Father, Son, and What?

You would think that we would not miss the rest of the story. Face it. When John the Baptist predicted the appearing of his successor, the one whose sandals he was unworthy to untie, he did not promise, "He shall die for your sins." John knew that Jesus had come for more than that. The Baptist did not promise, "He will rise triumphantly from the dead." John knew that the Savior's triumph would be greater even than that.

When introducing Jesus, John said of him, "He shall baptize you in . . ." Well, you know.

When Jesus predicted his own death, and when the disciples responded with dismay, he told them of what lay ahead. "I shall send . . . , who shall be with you." Who?

Then again, after Jesus' death and resurrection, while speaking with the bewildered disciples, he exhorted them, "Remain here until you are clothed with . . ." With what, indeed?

Then when Peter preached to what was about to become the first collection of converts, who would bring immediate growth to the faith community of about 10,000 percent, he said, "Believe and be baptized and you will receive the gift of . . ."

You would think we would get the story complete. You would think that believers would understand in hindsight what great significance the scriptures place upon the third member of the Trinity for whose coming Jesus was preparing the way. But no. For most Christians, the Trinity may rightly be named "Father, Son, and What?"

Not for Lack of Consideration

Every Christian knows the name of the third member of the Trinity. All Christians have asked curious questions about the one that completes the Godhead. But the answers generally have been incomplete and unsatisfying.

Some folks have asked pressing questions to understand better this enigma within the divine personality. Some have had experiences that have pressed them into shouting their answers.

Around the fringes of the historic church has orbited a movement of enthusiastic Christians claiming they do know—and have experienced—the rest of the story. *Enthusiastic* is the word. For centuries, major theologians have derided them by calling them "the Enthusiasts." In recent years titles like "Holy Rollers" and "Pentecostals" have come to the fore.

The common message among Pentecostals is that the third member of the Trinity must be experienced with miracle-working power. They point out that the Greek name of the person, *pneuma,* is used interchangeably with the word *dynamis,* from which we derive the modern word dynamite. Many of the early believers, especially the writer of the book of Acts, were thunderstruck by the explosive miraculous impact made by, upon, and through those early believers who took seriously this completion of the gospel story.

Then again, many believers have found this addition to the traditional gospel to ring hollow. They have felt that the worship style of such groups lacks the dignity worthy of a holy God. They have found the proclamation of Christ superseded by the proclamation of personal experience. In fact, personal "words from God" have been given precedence over the holy "Word of God." Sheer volume and flamboyance often have built huge audiences. In short, the freewheeling style of Pentecostalism lacks lasting appeal for many of those wanting to know the rest of the story.

The Pentecostals do have part of the rest of the story to tell. Jesus did say, "You shall receive power" in reference to this third member of the Trinity who was to come upon the disciples. It's just that Jesus seems to have had more in mind than is proclaimed by the enthusiasts.

Then again, more mainstream traditions have not been silent on the third member of the Trinity. In an era when the state church had been corrupted by its power and privilege, revivalist John Wesley preached long and hard of the transforming impact this one brings. He urged his followers to set their sights on the moral character exemplified by Christ himself. "If Christ could live a sinless life, then Christ in you can as well," so his message went. The message of sanctification led his band of followers to be labeled as the Holiness Movement.

Wesley recognized in the scriptures that sanctification did not result simply from willpower. Even though his followers called themselves Methodists, he offered no specific methods or programs of disciplines to make a person holy. Rather, he preached that holiness begins with a miraculous infilling of God's power. Holiness has to be a gift transacted by the third member of the Trinity. *Perfect holiness,* also known as *total sanctification,* became his personal pursuit. It also became the carrot on the end of the stick in all his preaching.

That preaching launched one of the largest Christian movements around the world. Ironically, though, few of today's Methodists would recognize Wesley's message were he to show up on a Sunday to preach it. The message of holiness, lofty as it is, does not gain a wide audience in a time when people's sins are too easily exposed. Too many Elmer Gantrys, portraying themselves as preachers of moral purity, have been caught in shameful misdeeds. In a world replete with evidence to support Paul's indictment, "All have sinned and fallen short of the glory of God," even the pursuit of holiness has been brushed aside.

That's too bad. What's also too bad is the fact that the message of total sanctification—even when proclaimed with the passion of Wesley himself—does not complete the story. The scriptures do not really hold forth the likelihood of reaching total perfection in this life.

The Reformed, or Calvinist, churches have never held forth the Methodist ideal of perfection, yet they have proclaimed the sanctifying power of the third member of the Trinity. Indeed, for all the credit given John Calvin for unfolding the message of grace, he actually devotes the largest block of pages in his *Institutes of the Christian Religion* to the subject of the third member of the Trinity.

For Calvin, the message of grace is one that not only captures the heart of the unbeliever. It also works a transforming work within the believer's life to make the person more like Christ. Though he held forth no hope of complete holiness in this life, he did proclaim that progress in grace fosters greater conformity to the will of God, as God's presence within empowers the individual. Moreover, the work of this member of the Godhead joins the believer into the larger body of believers, enabling all to experience God's word as it is proclaimed by teaching elders, who themselves are imbued by the presence of God.

Nevertheless, the story was never completely told by Calvin. In his day, freewheeling enthusiasts so pressed their point that he opted to proclaim a more cautious outlook toward the experience of God's presence. He did not want to presume greater comprehension of God than was appropriate for a sin-bent human. Discretion being the better part of valor, he hesitated to claim for himself the full expression of God's presence, as did the apostles of Jesus' day.

Evangelicals also have proclaimed the work of this divine successor to Jesus' life and ministry. Their evangelistic work long has depended upon his promise: "You shall receive power when" this one "comes upon you, and you shall be my witnesses . . . to the uttermost part of the earth." The evangelistic task can be effective only as empowered by God. Yet that's not the whole of the story either.

Other Christian traditions, from Roman Catholic to Baptist, make reference to this enigmatic member of the Godhead, but seemingly as an afterthought, an appendix to the real story. Most have been scared away from the rest of the story.

Then again, it has not been only some conservative traditions that have claimed the third member of the Trinity as their patron saint. Radical revisionists also insist that their new ideas are inspired by this member of the Godhead. Although Jesus' words are concrete and the Father's role is definitively clear, our neglect of the extensive biblical teaching on the third member of the Trinity has opened the door to all kinds of fanciful teachings being attributed to his or her inspiration.

New theologies, from liberationist to feminist, arise on the same basis. New ethics and immoralities are justified on the same basis. Self-anointed leaders promote their revelations on the same basis. All moorings for belief are eschewed in favor of the wildly, radically inclusive, subjectively interpreted third member of the Trinity. "The letter kills; the . . . gives life," so they quote. The claimed inspiration of the presence of God gives license to all kinds of belief that disregards the will of God already revealed in scripture.

Is it no wonder that the rest of the story does not get told? Unfortunately, the net result is that the Trinity still remains Father, Son, and What's-Its-Name.

Even in Biblical Studies . . .

Numerous students of scripture have readily recognized the need to tell the complete story regarding the fullness of the Godhead. They have recognized that the third member of the Trinity is not an afterthought in scripture, even if treated that way in the church.

They have read again and again of the impact made by God's presence in people's lives throughout Holy Writ. But attempts to string together the episodes in scripture have met much scholarly resistance.

Given that scripture claims to be inspired by God, by implication that means there is one ultimate Author. By further implication, that should lead to one central unifying theme intended to be conveyed by that Author. From those assumptions the Reformers inferred that all scripture is built around the theme of God's covenant of redemptive grace. All of the Old Testament was seen as the preparation and the New Testament as the fulfillment of such a theme, with the climax coming at the cross and resurrection of Christ. Classic texts like *The Unfolding Drama of Redemption* and *The Scarlet Cord* not only summarized the faith for scholars; they popularized a coherent grasp of the gospel for the laity.

However, over the past two centuries scholars have paid closer attention to the particularity of each book by each individual author. In the process, they have become increasingly uncomfortable with the pattern of mapping out books of the Bible as if they comprise a singular guided tour leading from a singular starting point to a singular destination. Too many texts of the scriptures just don't fit the simplistic mapping that has been popularly subscribed.

In this century, the whole study of biblical theology, that is, salvation history, has fallen into neglect. In spite of the yearning from the pews to provide an integrated grasp of the whole message of scripture, most biblical scholars shun any such attempt. Parts of the story can be told, but a continuous threading together of the story is rejected in most scholarly circles.

So the rest of the story goes untold, and the church wonders why it no longer is turning the world upside down. Indeed, the church of Jesus Christ hungers to understand who it is, and Christians long to grasp the vitality of faith experienced by the church of the apostles.

Can the Story Be Told at All?

There are signs of hope. In the world of scholarship, some biblical scholars are calling for a rebirth of biblical theology. In so doing, many, such as Samuel Terrien, are now declaring that there does exist a common denominator, a central theme that weaves all the Bible's books into one book. This central theme is to be found within the untold story of the third member of the Trinity. Terrien asserts that "the reality of the presence of God stands at the center of biblical faith."[3]

A strange thing is going on among theologians. They are writing about the Trinity. After decades of broad speculations exploring fringe ideas, many of the world's leading scholars are back to studying the identity of God as revealed in scripture. Could it be that all three members of the Trinity will be adequately discussed?

In the world of spirituality, mainline denominational leaders are going on retreats to reclaim the experiential reality of personal faith. And folks in the pews are pressing their leaders to put up or shut up—that is, to unfold the whole counsel of God regarding the spiritual life—or watch their sanctuaries empty.

Still, the question begs attention. What about the rest of the story?

Well, that story can be told. It can be told in a way that is faithful to the original, intended meaning of each of the texts of scripture that help unfold the overall story. It can be told in a way that

---

3. Terrien, *The Elusive Presence,* xxvii.

reflects the best scholarship while being accessible to everyday believers. It can be told in a way that retains the dignity of traditional worship while elevating the passion and power evidenced in the enthusiast churches. It can be told in a way that glorifies the Godhead—all three persons. It can be told in a way that shows how the cross and resurrection accomplished their intended purposes. It can be told in a way that helps Christians to experience the spiritual life without losing their grip on the practical.

So What Gives?

Today, most believers have found themselves standing in the midst of the gaping crowd asking, "Are these folks drunk with new wine?"

Unfortunately, the response they have been given has been, "Yes, they are."

Or they've been told, "Oh, they're just a part of a passing fad."

Or they've been told, "They're a bunch of fanatics."

What they—what *we* have needed to hear is, "These are not drunk, as you suppose, for it is only nine o'clock in the morning. No, *this is what was spoken through the prophet Joel: 'In the last days it will be, God declares, that I will pour out my Spirit . . .'*"

You see, the rest of the story is titled "Holy Spirit."

The turning point of history was not the cross or the resurrection. It was Pentecost. On Pentecost, Holy Spirit came with power. Accordingly, Pentecost marks the climax of the biblical narrative. Yes, the Pentecostals are correct on that point. On Pentecost, Holy Spirit infused believers with holiness. The Methodists and Reformers are correct on that point. On Pentecost, Holy Spirit launched the proclamation of the gospel, as evangelicals declare, and empowered the work of ministry, as Catholics claim.

Yet Holy Spirit did one thing more basic and essential than all those religious traditions collectively have proclaimed. But to understand the essential impact of the gift of Holy Spirit, one needs to hear the whole story as it unfolds in the whole biblical narrative. We need to understand what it was that prophets like Joel were promising. We need to grasp what David, and Moses before him, experienced in anticipation of the gift that would someday be given to "whosoever will." We need to hear with the ears of Abram and Sarai the invitation held forth by God. We need to feel with Adam and Eve the horror of their tragic loss. It is only as the story unfolds, and as we follow the clues throughout the biblical story, that we can finally apprehend—and be apprehended by—the full-orbed message that makes up the rest of the story.

And so we begin in the garden.

2

The Desperation of Independence

"*T*hey heard the sound of the Lord walking in the garden in the cool of the day."

Imagine the moment. The ultimate Being, the Sovereign of the universe walking toward them.

"They heard the sound of the Lord walking in the garden in the cool of the day."

Imagine the sound. Could it have been the menacing thuds of enemy footsteps? Perhaps it was the crackling of dry leaves and the snapping of breaking branches. Or was it simply the quiet blowing of a gentle breeze?

We cannot know for sure what they heard. But they knew *who* they heard. The sound, whether thundering or whispering, was familiar to them. They knew the sound of God because they knew the friendship of God. The first woman and man were created in God's garden.

Humanity had its beginnings in close fellowship with its Creator. The book of Genesis conveys that reality vividly: the man, the woman, and the Lord walking together in the garden in the cool of the day. No doubt the writer intends us to visualize and feel the setting. To commune with God meant sharing a lush locale at the best time of the day, perhaps early in the new morning or in the stillness just before dusk. Meetings with God felt like a refreshing breeze blowing on a balmy day, like hiking through the woods on a path just wide enough for the husband, the wife, and their Friend to walk side by side.

It seems strange to think of God being found in such a specific place and time. Bible teachers long have taught about the Judeo-Christian God being in all places at all times. They speak of the omnipresence of God. In a general sense, they are correct. God is everywhere. The Spirit-Presence that hovered over the waters like a transcendent dove throughout the creative process hovers over all today.

However, the prevailing picture given in the Bible is of a God who settles in one place at any one given time. Seemingly, in some dimension, God has localized the divine Presence in particular places for particular reasons.

The most obvious locale, God's hometown, is heaven. "I saw the Lord seated on a throne, high and exalted, and the train of his robe filled the temple," says the prophet Isaiah (6:1 NIV).

God has been known to set up a dwelling place in special earthly locations, too. Bethel, which means "house of God," is so named because it is where Jacob wrestled through the night with the divine Presence. Sinai, called the mountain of God, provided a holy ground for Moses to encounter God—and a place where Elijah would later flee to seek out the voice of the Lord. The tabernacle and its successor, the Temple, provided God handmade residences, dwelling places for the Spirit-Presence near the people.

Adam and Eve enjoyed the privilege of walking with God in such a place—perhaps the best of all such dwellings—the garden of God. Their conversational stroll through the woods was repeated often in those days of innocence. Our imaginations can run wild pondering the topics discussed, the lessons learned, the tenderness shown. Theirs was the ultimate privilege—one that others would yearn to experience for generations to come. However, the privilege would prove to be out of reach to their children and grandchildren. This incredible birthright Adam and Eve would squander. They would trade it away.

They "heard the sound of the LORD God as he was walking in the garden in the cool of the day" (Gen. 3:8 NIV). This time the sound took on a tone different than before. The sound always had been a pleasant one. This time it sounded awful. No, the sound itself did not register any greater decibels or higher pitch. The difference was in the hearing.

Adam and Eve had committed the inexcusable sin. God had given them free rein in the garden. "Anything you want to eat you may," said the Master. "Name the animals, enjoy the fruits and vegetables, be fruitful and multiply." Those command-promises were happily received. There was just one thing they were not to do: "Do not eat of this one tree. If you do, that day you will die."

At issue was the question of authority. The fruit tree was to serve as a test case for their willingness to abide by God's rules. The Creator had brought them into existence as God's offspring. Would the children love and respect their Creator-Father, or would they try to recast the relationship to their own mold? Would they grab for the possibility of being answerable to no one? Would they refuse to acknowledge God as their God?

Those questions were critical ones for the first humans. No such question had been posed to any other created being. All the plants and animals were preprogrammed to do just as created. They had no choice but to follow their inbuilt genetic rules and instincts. No debate, no discussion. However, to the highest being of the creation, a choice was being presented. The Creator would not program the man and woman to say, "I love you; I worship you," as if reading cue cards before a camera. The Lord wanted their love and worship but only by their choice, and that choice could be a true choice only if there were an alternative.

The serpent suggested just such an alternative: "Has God not told you that if you eat the fruit, you will not die? Did God not tell you that you shall become as gods?" In other words, has that Dictator-in-the-Sky hidden from you the fact that if you rebel, you will gain total autonomy—that you will be free to do as you please from now on?

It sounded so inviting. Why shouldn't I take charge of my own life? Who gives God the right to tell me what I can and cannot do? Those words have been echoed through the ages. Who are the British that they can tax our tea? What gives the city council the right to dictate how I decorate my front lawn? Who does my mother think she is that she dare tell me what to wear?

Probably most of us have imagined how much better the world would be had Adam and Eve not eaten of the fruit. If I were there, we've thought, I wouldn't have done it. Think again. Would we really have done better, we who treat the Declaration of Independence as the sixty-seventh book of the Bible? We not only would have eaten the forbidden fruit; we probably would have done so much quicker. We wouldn't even have taken the time to name the animals.

Well, they did eat. They took the fruit and ate of it. Suddenly they realized what they had done. They scrambled around to find leaves behind which they could hide their now-private parts. Isn't that the way it has been ever since? Sin heads for cover.

"They heard the sound of the Lord walking in the garden in the cool of the day." The sound was ominous. They knew that the veil of death had already befallen them. Their beloved Friend was coming, not for friendly conversation, but to mete out dreaded retribution.

Would they die that day? Well, no—not if you define death as the termination of heartbeats, the silencing of brainwaves. Rather, what befell them was a death of another kind. They died spiritually.

Curiously, the death they endured was the very thing they had desired. They sought autonomy. God gave them autonomy. They wanted to rule themselves. God gave them self-rule. They wanted to be free of God's domination. They would now answer to no one but themselves.

If you think about it, damnation to hell is just like that. Casting a person into hell is not a horrifyingly nasty act by a vengeful God. Hell's ultimate penalty consists merely in granting to people the autonomy in death that had been chosen in life. It is the act of granting a person the absolute freedom from God that was yearned for and pursued throughout one's years.

God gave Adam and Eve their freedom. God set them loose outside the garden. That's not so bad, they might have thought. We can go back for a visit from time to time. But then they noticed huge creatures standing by the garden's gate. They quickly deduced that these were angels, sentinels assigned to guard the entrance to the garden. They were to prevent the man and woman from making any attempted return. Banished, Adam and Eve could not go back.

Such a wall of protection did make sense. There was room in God's garden for only one God. A rival god would bring clashing, contention, and war. Such a war could only wipe out the highest of God's created beings. Rather than face such a battle, God set the man and woman free to provide for and rule over themselves.

Banishment was a word that broke God's heart. That was not what the Creator envisioned in the creative process. Relationship, closeness and tenderness, having an outlet on which to lavish the immeasurable divine love—that was the Lord's desire.

When I served as pastor of Trinity Church in Satellite Beach, Florida, the one task I detested most was that of banishing the skateboarders. The grounds around the church buildings are a skateboarder's paradise. Hundreds of feet of smooth sidewalks, wide stairways, banisters, block walls, and curbs marked the property as the best skateboarding venue in town. For a long time we welcomed the skateboarders. We'd serve snacks to these mostly unchurched teens—many of them skinheads—and share the gospel with them regularly. Linda, the church secretary, would preach and teach Bible studies to them, gradually breaking down their cool defensiveness. A few prayed to receive Christ into their lives.

However, they eventually lived up to their own teenage version of the human condition. They bent and twisted banisters that had stood in their concrete foundations for decades. They cursed and swore at adults who ventured by. They found a way up to the roof to skateboard down its 30 degree incline. We began finding evidence of drug use, including bottles of glue sniffed dry. The insurance company warned us that any injury could produce a lawsuit costing millions, and it would not back us if we did not do our best to chase off the kids. Frightened parents of our preschoolers were starting to pull their children out of the program, just to avoid these hoodlums. The police urged us to shut them down.

Then one day while I was out of town, racial tensions boiled over in the high school, and a gang war was staged. Can you guess where the youth chose to fight? Here they came, dozens of enraged teens egged on by their parents, hungry for the sight of blood—just as the sixty children attending our preschool were being dismissed. With the help of several police officers, Linda was finally able to disperse the crowd (not without the worst resistance coming from the well-to-do parents of the skinheads!), and nobody was physically harmed. But nothing could be the same hereafter.

Reality set in. These kids whom I had grown to love—in a different sort of way—had to go. They were destruction on wheels. This place set aside as a sanctuary for the worship of God could not be given over to the reckless vandalism and violence that their uncurbed human nature was wreaking. A special elders' meeting produced a clear-cut ruling. A new task was added to the pastor's job description—banishing all skateboarders.

Even now it deeply disturbs me to think that somehow God's turf must be protected from people rather than made fully accessible to even the worst among us. But that's how it is today.

That's how it was in the beginning, too. Adam and Eve had to go. They were destruction in fig leaves.

The first man and woman soon discovered the downside of freedom. Independence implies separation. Autonomy brings alienation. They realized that on that day they surely had died. They had cut themselves off from the One who is the tree of life, in whose presence there had been fullness of joy.

Quickly the natural consequences of alienation emerged, and the effects of the sin were blistering: pain in childbirth, domination of one another in conflicts, the need to toil with an uncooperative natural order, and the threat of returning as dust to the ground. Other consequences of their sin soon followed: drunkenness, unfaithfulness, violence, even murder. Yet, horrific as these acts were, the ultimate loss was their squandering the presence of God. They felt desperately alone. They were cut off.

In God's mercy, that forbidden tree granted the humans a basic understanding of good and evil, an inner sense of conscience with which they might maintain a degree of order. The possession of a conscience is the silver lining on the cloud of humanity's fall.

Nevertheless, they would live forever with flawed character. People of faith have often wondered about the extent of negative moral flaws that have been passed on to the children of Eve and Adam. Are we born guilty because, as our representative mother and father, they acted on our behalf just as we would have acted?

Or are we born weakened, now more inclined to sin? Or both? One thing is for sure. We were born outside the garden. The original sin had geographical effects. Being separated from God means being cut off from the source of goodness and blessedness. Inevitably, a life-style of sin-living results, and, in turn, each act of sin further expands the gaping chasm dividing us from God's presence.

It was from the dimension of such a wonder-inspiring presence that Adam and Eve had now been banished. They had refused the one prerequisite to enjoying such communion. They refused to acknowledge God as *their* God.

Can you imagine making a decision of such lasting eternal significance? The first couple's decision was irreversible. They could not go back. The decision would continue to haunt them and their children for all time.

We make decisions all the time. Some of those decisions define a life. A politician is haunted by poorly chosen friendships made decades ago. An unemployed single mother looks back to the decision she made as an eighteen-year-old for romance over education, knowing that poverty is now tracking her like a bloodhound. As an airplane high above a football stadium carries the banner saying, "Rachel, will you marry me?" all present witness a decision being made by a man and a woman that they will live out "till death us do part."

Decisions are made by each human mind with a speed and frequency that rivals that of the supercomputers. Moment by moment we decide which way to look, what task to do, what plans to make, what friends to engage in conversation, what attitudes to adopt, what feelings to feel. Yes, even our feelings are things we choose.

It's hard to imagine, though, making a decision of such enormous impact as was made by Adam and Eve. The fate of the world was held in their grip. One false bite and poof! It's all over.

What about us? Is there any way to get out of their decision? Can we, somehow, get back into the garden of God? Is there any way back to Eden?

Unfortunately, there was no such way for Adam and Eve. For centuries there would be no possibility of it. In fact, throughout the Old Testament era, we are afforded only glimpses of Spirit-filled living—as experienced in intermittent ways by a mere handful of God's people. But if we would sneak a peek into the future, look ahead to the days of the apostles and listen to their preaching, we will hear them making a clearly presented invitation: "Repent and be baptized, every one of you, in the name of Jesus Christ so that your sins may be forgiven. And you will receive the gift of the Holy Spirit" (Acts 2:38 NIV).

We who live in the days following the apostles' preaching are afforded the opportunity to make a final decision, too. It also is a final decision with eternal consequences. Like that of Adam and Eve, this decision is irreversible. There's one incredible difference, however. Their one failed decision led to their banishment. Our one correct decision brings the fullness of Holy Spirit into our lives—forever.

Yes, one foolish decision can ruin a life. But one right decision can resurrect a death. A man finds a lottery ticket in a gutter and wins $7 million (it really happened in Florida!). A quarterback shouts out a change of play just before the ball is snapped, and in a moment of time he heaves the conference-winning touchdown. Yet those good decisions pale in comparison to the one decision to welcome the Spirit of God into our lives.

To be sure, we can't receive what is not available. For centuries Holy Spirit was cordoned off from humanity. Living the Spirit had to begin with Holy Spirit being made available, being poured out upon us, and drawing us to faith. That was God's job to accomplish. But whether we actually experience the Spirit-filled life depends upon one decision that can be made by nobody but us. It is as straightforward as was Adam and Eve's. The one difference, as we have said, is that they had everything to lose, whereas we have everything to gain. The decision? To say "Yes" to God.

"In all thy ways acknowledge him . . ."

That decision is one that fundamentally begins with God's love extended. That love was expressed in ultimate terms—the sending of Jesus, God's Son, to live as a human and to die a criminal's death in order to save us. That love became accessible when, after the resurrection and ascension, Jesus sent forth the presence of God, Holy Spirit, to live in all who would acknowledge Jesus as Lord and Savior. That in turn leads to the decision each of us must make.

Is living the presence of Holy Spirit what you really want? Do you want to walk closely with God? You are reading this book, so you probably do. If so, then the decision is direct. Such a decision means reversing the action taken by our Eden ancestors. It means acknowledging one God and desiring to obey that one God. It presumes that you are willing to relinquish self-control and autonomy in order to put God's will before your own.

In some churches a few moments are set aside for the worshipers to express their faith, usually by reciting the Apostles' Creed. Such declarations of faith give the believers an opportunity to testify to both the content and the intensity of the faith they hold. One simple affirmation comes in a question-and-answer format. The minister asks, "Friends, who is your God?" The congregation responds, "The Father who loves us, that is our God. The Son who saves us, that is our God. The Spirit who indwells us, that is our God. One God in three persons, that is our God."

Whether expressed in the same words or similar ones, there comes a distinct time to decide who is to be our God. Moses and the children of Israel could have moaned and whined for another century about being enslaved. Or they could, that Passover day, pack their bags, leave their familiar surroundings, and head out to the land God would show them. They had to decide to take a journey with God or simply to continue to wallow in their sub-potential life-styles.

Accordingly, there comes a time for every man and woman to decide. Who is your God? If you would like to change gods from the wrong one to the Right One, a simple prayer can say it. Perhaps you'd like to pray such a prayer:

Dear Lord Jesus, I know that I am a sinner and am separated from God. I believe that you died for my sins, so please forgive me for living separate from you. I now invite you to take control of my life, and I welcome Holy Spirit into my life. I want to trust you as Savior and follow you as Lord, in the fellowship of your church. Amen.

Do you know what happens when such a decision is whispered as a prayer? All heaven breaks loose. Every sin you have ever committed—every act that ratified Adam and Eve's rejection of God—is immediately forgiven. You stand before the Holy One as if you had never sinned. Your relationship with God is no longer merely that of created to Creator but as a daughter or son to a loving heavenly Father. Ownership of your heart and soul is taken by God from the serpent's cohorts. A process of transforming your bad habits into good is set in motion. Healing of damaged emotions is initiated. Most of all, the presence of God, Holy Spirit, takes up residence within you, never to leave.

The decision is irrevocable. Like Adam and Eve's "No" to God, our "Yes" to God is a final decision. Unlike their "No," our "Yes" brings us into a direct, connected relationship that is unbreakable, indivisible, and eternal.

Can that be? Can it be that the Spirit will never depart? What if you should disobey God? Odds are that you will sin in thought, word, or deed daily. What if you turn your back on God? God will turn with you.

Surely the minister who has compromised all integrity to fleece naive, unsuspecting followers out of their money in order to buy mansions and limousines must be forsaken by the God of holiness. Certainly pompous, self-exalting egoists have pushed out the Presence. Yet even to them Jesus says, "I will never leave you or forsake you."

This promise is graphically expressed in a scolding given by the apostle Paul. Apparently, word had circulated back to the church leader that Christians in Corinth were engaging in pagan acts of worship, including having relations with temple prostitutes. He was horrified! "The body is not meant for sexual immorality, but for the Lord, and the Lord for the body," says Paul. His point is clear. There must be no hint of such immorality among the Christians.

However, what happens to the ones who already are guilty of such wanton debauchery? What if the body, filled with the Lord, is united to a prostitute? The Lord could never abide there. Surely God would have to depart. The Spirit would have to flee, or so it would seem. But no, that's not what Paul says. "Do you not know that your bodies are members of Christ himself? Shall I then take the members of Christ and unite them with a prostitute? Never!" Horrified as he is about such behavior, the deterrent he raises to the Corinthians is not the threat of divine abandonment but the shock of dragging the Lord into such sin.

The real reason not to sin, says Paul, is that you thereby unite the presence of Holy Spirit to the presence of wickedness. He crystallizes his point: "He who unites himself with the Lord is one with him in spirit. . . . Do you not know that your body is a temple of the Holy Spirit, who is in you, whom you have received from God? You are not your own; you were bought at a price. Therefore honor God with your body" (1 Cor. 6:17–20 NIV).

Even under the worst circumstances and in the midst of our worst behavior, the Presence once received abides in us forever without interruption.

Thus it all boils down to a decision—a once-for-all decision to have Jesus as Lord, God as Father, and Holy Spirit as Indweller. It is saying "Yes" to God. Unfortunately, Adam and Eve failed in their decision, and "all we like sheep" have followed suit. But thanks to the availability of the Spirit through Jesus' work and by the power of our decision to say "Yes" to God, we can enter into that Spirit-filled life.

Moving on from the essential, irrevocable decision demands further decisions. A choice of such eternal consequences needs daily ratification. That is to say, Spirit living is like marriage living. The marriage covenant is entered once to last till death. However, to enjoy its benefits, each partner must daily give and receive conversation, affection, and love. So too, although the Spirit-Presence is given once and for all, the Spirit-filled life needs to be renewed daily. Deciding daily to converse with God, to express gratitude, to serve, to obey: such are the decisions to be made that enable us to enjoy the full benefits of the gift of Holy Spirit.

The one essential activity that renews our relationship with God and enables us to enjoy the benefits of the Presence is that of the exercise of our faith. In a sense, that seems strange. An employer does not expect employees to believe in him; they simply must do as they are told. A mother does not ask children to believe in her but simply to learn and grow as guided by her. A spouse seeks not so much faith as love. Yet God expects belief.

Faith enables us to lay hold of the unseen and unperceived Presence. When Holy Spirit seems out of reach and when we seem to be walking blindly, it is belief in God's promises and presence that provides the Seeing Eye dog to lead us. When the feeling of walking with God in the cool of the day fades into the feeling of walking alone in the frozen tundra, it is faith that warms and renews and restores our confidence and communication with the One whose pace is invisibly shadowing our every step.

One couple experienced the cold chill of desperate loneliness. They had heard the voice of God and had known the friendship of God. But their conversations with the Almighty were like a few tiny islands scattered across a vast sea. They were brief and infrequent—about once or twice a decade. For years they and their offspring would have to find something else on which to depend, something other that the close feelings of God's presence to keep them going.

They discovered a secret. They—that is, Abraham and Sarah—discovered a key. Thousands of years after the fateful decision of Adam and Eve, Abraham and Sarah encountered and responded to the Presence in a different way. They thereby earned the titles "father and mother of faith." Instructed by God's promises and buoyed by a keen memory, they learned to put their trust in God.

Accordingly, let us turn our attention to their story to learn how to live—by faith—the presence of the Spirit when the Spirit seems miles away.

"Help Thou My Unbelief"

*R*ecently I asked a crowd of several hundred people, "How many here have ever felt close to God?" To my happy surprise, every single person raised a hand. I followed with a second question, "How many here have ever felt far away from God?" To no surprise, every single person again raised a hand. Several raised both hands. Many nodded their heads in a conceding it's-true-but-I-wish-it-weren't sort of a way.

If you've ever felt that closeness, you've found it easy to trust God. But if you've felt that empty alienation, you've also found it hard to trust God.

The close feeling can be so effervescent. You hum along during a performance of Handel's *Messiah* or tap your feet at a Michael W. Smith concert. You join hands in a prayer circle or whisper "Help her, Lord," as your friend shares publicly her spiritual journey. You experience the unexcelled thrill of praying with someone to accept Christ. Such experiences can generate an intensity of feeling that makes every nerve quiver. But when the feeling goes, watch out.

I was fifteen years old when I welcomed Christ into my life. I had been invited to attend a teen prayer meeting held Tuesday evenings at a nearby nondenominational church. When the small-group discussion turned the spotlight on me, the lone outsider, the leader asked if I wanted to receive Jesus into my life. I had no idea what he meant, but being impressed with the joy that decorated the faces around me, I responded haltingly, "Well, uh, sure." I prayed as he suggested, repeating the words after him.

Suddenly, and without warning, I felt a tingling surge up

my spine. I was overwhelmed with the sense of God-in-me. All evening long I felt airborne, immersed in Tinkerbell's fairy dust.

For months, the feelings swirled around in me. Whenever they would begin to fade, they would be renewed by inbreakings of the power of God. I asked God for things in prayer and received them just as requested. I sensed God speaking to me, giving clear answers to my fuzzy questions. In turn, at every Tuesday prayer gathering I testified glowingly about the things God had done in my life that week.

After ten months of such testimonies, Phil, our Tuesday Night Prayer Rap leader, took me aside to tell me—in as gracious a tone as he could muster—"You don't need to give a testimony every week." In others words, the prayer meeting could survive without me. Or more to the point, "We're getting sick of hearing you jabber on." I was brought down to size.

He had more to say. From his towering height and vulture-dark eyes (he could have played a part in a Stephen King movie), he put his hand on my shoulder. I braced for the worst. "Be prepared," he warned in a soft but ominous tone. "God has a way of pulling out the rug from under us. Probably, before too long, your prayers won't be answered as impressively as they have been, and you may not feel God's presence anymore."

Just as he had warned, my spiritual feelings dried up. Immediately. The white-hot fervor of excitement turned to a northern chill, and my prayers bounced off the ceiling. The Presence with whom I had become so friendly had lost the verve, or so it felt.

Over the months that followed, Phil, reeling with guilt for stifling my enthusiasm, still called on me from time to time to testify. But I'd have to reach to find something to say. Either I would tell an old tale about last year's miracle, or I'd say something nice on God's behalf, often stretching the truth to try to make God look good—as if God needed my help.

God has a way of blacking out the electrical charge fueling our spiritual passion. God is notorious for turning off the floodwaters of blessings.

How are we to live in the *afterwards* of salvation? How are we to live the presence of the Spirit when the Spirit feels miles away?

God's answer boils down to a single word. It is the one word that summarizes the first essential of Christian practice. No, it is not *obedience*. True as it is that obedience is the opposite of what Adam and Eve did, just obeying will not turn things around. No, it is not *love* either. Central as love is to the behavior God desires, it does not provide a starting point for our walk with God. Moreover, we are powerless to love unless empowered by something else. Love is a by-product.

What God requires of us is *faith*—which brings us to a man and a woman, Abraham and Sarah.

It seems strange that the New Testament writers consistently showcase Abraham as the ultimate model of godly faith. Mentioned seventy-two times in the New Testament, second only to Moses, Abraham is portrayed as the ultimate example of faith. True, when called to leave his home country to go to a place God was preparing for him, he packed up his family and ventured out. However, when visiting in Egypt, this man of faith and power told his wife to pretend she was his sister, lest the lustful Egyptians should harm him to claim her. Would not faith have courageously protected one's loved one? Would not faith at least have trusted God for one's *own* survival?

On the positive side, when Abraham was presented the promise of being the father of a nation created to be God's own people, he believed God—so much so that he was justified by his faith. He was certified to be in a right relationship with God. However, having judged that his wife, Sarah, could not carry the promised offspring, he impregnated his servant girl, Hagar, so she could bear him a son. Is that an example of trust toward God?

We can appreciate the impatience Abraham must have felt, knowing that he must await God's timing to have a child. Would you want to be raising a rambunctious two-year-old if you were 101 years old? Nevertheless, as the model of faith, he is less than impressive.

On the other hand, faith does reach a high watermark on one later occasion; that is, at a time when Abraham's feelings must have been at their dry-river-bed lowest. After having fathered the promised son, Isaac, and after years of subsequent silence from God, he heard the Lord speak, "Abraham, take your son to Mount Moriah, to the place I will show you and sacrifice him there to me."

"What? Can this be? Sacrifice my son to God?" We do not know exactly what Abraham thought, but we can imagine.

Who of us would happily offer our child as a sacrifice to be killed in honor of God? Admittedly, a few well-intentioned parents have thought about ways to do in their junior-high-aged kids. Teens can test the limits of one's self-control. Nevertheless, the final solution is too horrifying even to consider. In fact, we arrest and imprison people who do such things.

Yet what did Abraham do? He got up the next day to do what God had commanded. In fact, he got up early. Now I don't know about you, but I would have slept in the next morning. I would have been in no hurry to do as God had commanded me.

How could Abraham have thought to do such a thing? Would not the parental instinct to protect his child have overcome his desire to please and obey God? But he did as God instructed and even rose early in the morning to do so. Why? How? The answer is simple. Abraham remembered.

He had a clear memory of what God had said and done with him. He remembered God's promise of a child, and he remembered how God had provided him a son at the hoary age of ninety-nine years. God had come through before. God could come through again.

More specifically, Abraham remembered how God had responded years before to his question, "How will I know these things will come to pass?" When God had promised offspring numbering the stars of the sky and the sand of the sea, Abram had wanted to believe, but he was incredulous. The promise seemed farfetched, so he asked God for some assurance.

God's response was rather strange by twentieth-century standards. God told Abram (at the time, Abraham was known by the shorter name) to gather a collection of animals. On cue, Abram then cut each animal in half, lengthwise, from the nose to the tail. He made two piles of the half-animals and then fell into a deep sleep, during which he heard God warn of the coming years of Abram's descendants' enslavement in Egypt.

Then after the sun fell behind the western horizon, Abram saw a fire burning out of the top of an earthen pot, sending off a thick dark plume of smoke. As he watched, the fiery pot paraded in suspended animation through the two piles of animals; the path outlined a figure eight.

Strange symbolism! But this was God's way of bringing Abram into a covenant-guaranteed interpersonal relationship. This formal ritual was a way of transacting an agreement akin to doing a closing on the purchase of a house or to signing a contract to play for a basketball team. Both partners were making promises. Both were being entitled to a set of expectations. And, as with any contract or covenant, sanctions for failing to fulfill the commitment were being enumerated as well.

In this ancient covenant-making ritual, the dance of the firepot among the split carcasses brought together the two separate piles of flesh, symbolizing God's intention to unite with Abram. God was entering into a generations-long relationship with Abraham (the elongated name resulting from the name of God—Yahweh—being merged with Abram's). God said, "You will be my people, and I will be your God."

In addition, such symbolism was God's way of declaring on oath: "May I be split open dead if I do not keep my promise." But covenant making, by its very nature, necessitates sanctions for lack of fulfillment. Just as the modern marital-covenant-breaker pays the price of the loss of property and personal partnership, so too the ancient covenant-breaker paid, but with the ultimate penalty—death. Do you remember the old line, "Cross my heart, hope to die?" That expression echoes the ancient oath-sanction covenant.

God had cut a covenant with Abram.

Years later, as he crawled out of bed in the predawn blackness, Abraham believed. He believed because he remembered the covenant. God had been faithful so far. God would be faithful still.

Abraham dressed, gathered a pile of wood, and took his son to the mountain to which God had directed him. Somehow he knew in his heart that God would come through. So he wondered as he walked. Perhaps God will provide another son to be the bearer of the family name after Isaac's untimely death. Perhaps God's mind will change about the sacrifice. Perhaps God has something else in mind. What Abraham did know was that some way, somehow, God would provide, because God had entered an ever-lasting covenant with him. God would fulfill the covenant.

Faith works that way. It begins with memory. Remembering. Faith can recall the time when a desperate prayer was met with an incredible miracle. Faith can recall the time when you felt so close to God that nothing and no one could distract you. Faith can remember the promises made by Jesus, and how he also cut a covenant in his blood so that you could and always would be God's own child. Faith can remember that the Spirit who made his home in your heart promised to stay—whether you feel him or not.

A popular praise song sings:

> All through the day, all through the night,
> Dwell in his promises, walk in his light.
> Darkness shall flee at his command.
> All through the day and night we're in his hand.

Walking in faith depends upon knowing and remembering and living in those promises.

So how can we cultivate such a faith? First, we need to educate our faith. Our faith for the future depends upon the promises of the past. You cannot believe the promises if you don't know what the promises say.

To be sure, there are many who would say that faith should not question and should not need knowledge. But that is not faith in the biblical sense. That is superstition. True faith is acting on the facts and truth of scripture as presented. It recognizes its need to be better informed. It hungers for wisdom. It asks a lot of questions.

In fact, it can be said that ignorance is just as much an enemy of faith as is disobedience. Repeatedly Jesus speaks to the fact that the people have not known the time of God's visitation, that they have acted in ignorance, and that—as he exclaimed on the cross, "they do not know what they are doing" (Luke 23:34 NIV).

D. L. Moody once said:

> If all the time that I have spent praying for faith was put together, it would be months. I thought that some day faith

was going to come down and strike me like lightning. But faith did not come. One day I read in the tenth chapter of Romans, "So then faith comes by hearing and hearing by the word of God." I had closed my Bible and prayed for faith. I now opened my Bible and began to read God's word, and faith has been growing ever since.

A learning faith is a growing faith.

Second, we need to struggle through our faith. If anything is learned from Abraham's experience, it is the fact that faith is not static. It faces its challengers. At times Abraham's faith soared, and at other times it crashed and burned. A growing faith, in fact, is a doubting faith. That is, true faith is always being challenged to doubt and, in the best of us, will fight through periods of deep doubt.

Faith is constantly being tested. By its very nature, faith challenges us to believe truths that cannot be scientifically verified, some of which can't even be visibly observed. In a day when signs and wonders are being experienced by some believers and when emotions are being stirred in many gatherings, we need to resist the temptation to base our faith primarily on such phenomena. God is far more real than any miracle or any feeling. As Thomas learned from Jesus, it is a blessing to be able to see and then believe, but more blessed are those who do not see yet still believe.

Third, we need to venture out in faith. True faith is a dangerous faith. It takes one's child up the mountain, risking every dream one has dreamed. It means asking for things that you would not have risked mentioning.

It is striking to read in the Gospels how Jesus raised the subject of prayer. So often, when he spoke of it, Jesus was almost pleading with the people to ask God for things. He sounded like a parent pleading with the children to accept their new bicycles and toys on Christmas morning. I've yet to see a child who needed such persuasion, yet adults seem to need persuading. Jesus did persuade; he urged us to ask God for things—lots of things.

His reasons, in part, for urging prayer were to encourage us to cultivate a conversational relationship with God as Person and to grow in gratitude toward God as Provider. His main reason, though, was simply to encourage our bold faith: "Ask for anything in my name and you shall receive it." He wanted us to have a faith that ventures beyond asking for daily bread into one that asks for employment, healing, and other needs that truly call for miraculous intervention.

Faith ventures out, taking the chance of believing that God can and will do something unpredictable. Faith ventures to believe that God is present regardless of the empirical evidence. The doubt that paralyzes is one that has grown deaf to the promises, that has given up against its challenges and has grown cautious. All the more, the doubt that kills is a doubt that loses touch with God's relationship to us.

Abraham remembered the relationship God introduced to him. It was a covenantal relationship. Accordingly, it was as secure as God's existence. Unfortunately, however, his relationship with God was not one of intimate communication. Their conversations were few and seldom. In contrast, the relationship to be made available centuries later because of the work of Jesus Christ would be marked by the continual, abiding, and loving presence of God in the lives of all believers. Although you and I may not be constantly aware of such a presence and may be able to disregard such a presence, the abiding, indwelling Holy Spirit is as sure a promise to believers today as was the promise of an ongoing destiny to Abraham. The key is in remembering. As we remember, so we believe.

Elmer Floyd is a close friend and fellow pastor. Not long ago, he shared with me the pain of a recent spiritual emptiness.

I am by nature a cheerleader, the ultimate optimist. My favorite line from a movie is from *Top Gun* when Tom Cruise says he wants to do Mach-2 with his hair on fire. The presence of God is at the center core of my being and makes that all happen. It is the intimate, ultimate relationship with God that just jazzes me for life.

But for two months I had a void. It all dried up. I could identify with David in the Psalms: "My God, my God, why have you forsaken me?" I kept going through the form and fashion, but it was emotionless and spiritless. It was cold, lonely, empty, void. I had lost my best Friend, my Encourager, my Supporter, and—worst of all—my God.

In the midst of all that, the senior pastor left town for a week, so I had to preach—not my favorite thing to do when I'm going through a spiritual desert. Nevertheless, I decided to develop a sermon on the temptations of Christ. As I studied those verses, I began to realize that the temptations were not directed at the physical nature of Christ; he really would have gained nothing by responding to Satan. But each temptation was for the purpose of causing him to doubt his relationship with God his Father. The bread was a temptation to doubt the sufficiency of God. The kingdom temptation was to doubt the authority of God. The pinnacle of the Temple temptation was to test the relationship with God—that God would intervene to save him from danger.

I have a habit of going to the beach to watch the sunrise. From Wednesday to Saturday of that week, the sky was cloudy and gray, the kind when you can't tell where the horizon ends and the sky begins. But on the Sunday I was to preach, I got there extra early. The sky was still dark but starting to hint of the coming dawn.

As I was praying and contemplating the sermon before me, I sensed God speaking to me. God said that I needed to listen to the sermon, that the sermon was intended for me. It was not just Jesus who had been tempted to distrust his relationship with his Father; I also was being tempted to distrust my relationship with my Father.

At just that moment, the sun came up in a brilliant ball of orange and red, backed by the teal blue of the sky. I wanted to dance on the boardwalk. The spark had returned. My God was real and present in the core of my being.

I realized that for the past four days the sun had been there. I just didn't see it. I also realized that God hadn't left me for those two months. I just didn't feel him. God had been there all along. I just needed to open my awareness to him.

Somehow Abraham kept that awareness open when he needed it most. With eyes darting left and right, and with ears peeled, he looked for God all the way up the mountain. Finally, with Isaac tied tightly to the makeshift altar, he drew his knife, held its shiny blade to his son's throat, and—

The voice of the angel called, "Abraham, Abraham." He had demonstrated his faith and proven his trust in God. God, in turn, provided a substitute sacrifice. God provided the ram.

On the mountain, Abraham learned the starting point for living the presence of the Spirit when the Spirit seems miles away. He learned to believe God.

Some years later, on another mountain, another man of faith fell upon the presence of the Spirit and came to know a bit more of the character of God. His name was Moses.

4

An Almost Perfect Fit

*T*he most heinous, scandalous atrocity of the twentieth century has been the horror of the Holocaust, the mass killing of millions of Jews, Roman Catholics, the mentally and physically handicapped, and others not deemed worthy of human life by Adolf Hitler and the Nazi soldiers. As if that were not evil enough, there is a scandal behind the atrocity, a horror within the horror. If you were to get to know one of those Nazi soldiers, visit within his home, and check out his wardrobe, you would discover on the buckle of his belt a brief inscription. In German it would read, *"Gott mit uns."* Take it to a translator, and with a shrug your bilingual helper would say, "Oh, I know that. Those words are a translation of an old Hebrew phrase, sometimes joined together into a single word. It's *'Im anu el.'* 'Immanuel.' You know. 'God with us.'" Immanuel. God is with us.

God with them? How can that be? Can we even conceive of the possibility that God could have been with the Nazis? Then again, could God be with the so-called white Christians in South Africa who for generations suppressed the rights of their black neighbors? Or could God have been with the so-called Christian Crusaders who battled the Muslims with sword during the Holy Wars of the Middle Ages? For that matter, could God be with all the winning football teams who huddle for a prayer of thanks as their defeated enemies walk off the field in dejection?

It would be easy to shout a loud "No!" Then again, whose sins are mild enough to be worthy of God's presence? Who is worthy enough to declare *Gott mit uns*—Immanuel—God is with us?

This is one reason why Protestant Christians commonly have neglected the teaching of the indwelling Holy Spirit. Having watched the Roman Catholic Church descend into periods of internal corruption, all the while claiming the Spirit's presence on their altars, the Reformers did not want to be guilty of a similar presumption. They did not want to treat God as a pendant hung from a neck chain. They did not want to squeeze God into a box of their own design. Instead of speaking of God as being immanent and available, they tended to speak of the Spirit in more elusive terms. Yes, they proclaimed that grace and forgiveness were a sure thing, every believer's inheritance. But they often spoke of the Spirit as one who comes near but always escapes our grasp.

Through the centuries a spirit of humility has prevailed in the church, promoting an image of the Spirit-Presence as beyond human indwelling.

However, the Bible speaks of God in a different way. God unites with people. God identifies with us: "I am the God of your fathers Abraham, Isaac, and Jacob." When you look back at the stories of these parents of Israel, it is hard to imagine that God would want to associate with them. Not everything they did was commendable. Not only did Abraham doubt God's trustworthiness; his son and grandson were known at times as men of violence and deception. Not everything they did was pure and ethical. They were not perfect model citizens. Could God be identified with their manipulations and deceptions?

God says, "I am the God of your fathers Abraham, Isaac, and Jacob." But is he also the God of Goering, Eichmann, and Himmler? Anybody who claims the title Christian? Something doesn't ring true at such a juncture.

Abraham or Moses? Paul or James?

Enter into the story a man by the name of Moses. His ancestor Abraham had met the Creator as the God of covenant. He had been *graced* into a relationship and thereby justified by faith. He knew God to be the Author of covenantal promises. But Moses met God on another basis. This same God said to him, "Take off your sandals. You are standing on holy ground." The God of the miraculous is also the God of holiness.

Moses took off his shoes, showing respect to a God who deserves honor. The theme of respect toward God's holiness pervades Moses' story. However, for modern-day students of the Bible, the whole Moses epic does not mix well with the rest of scripture. The teachings on holiness are commendable enough, but the New Testament seems to speak critically about the law and disciplines of Moses' day. Even in the Old Testament, his message seems to conflict with the free-grace message that emerges from the story of Abraham.

In truth, there runs throughout the word of scripture a tension between these two messages. On the one hand, we hear of God's covenant with Abraham, based upon grace-through-faith. On the other hand, we hear of God's covenant with Moses, seemingly based upon works. Abraham's relationship with God was unconditional, given simply as a gift. Moses' relationship with God appears to be conditional, based upon obedience to God's demands. Throughout the Old Testament these themes weave in and out.

David lives in the realm of grace, with God's love being bestowed upon him freely, in spite of himself. But then the prophets Samuel and Nathan come and point the finger at him: "Thou shalt do this. How dare you do that!"

To the prophet Hosea, God says, "Marry this harlot." Hosea was to be a living parable for the people, showing them how God's love continually floods over them like a tidal wave in spite of their prostituting themselves with other gods. But on the other hand, through the weeping prophet Jeremiah, God harshly judges the actions of the people, scolding them again and again.

Then there is poor Jonah, caught between grace and works. God commissions him to go to Nineveh to speak condemnation and judgment. "That's super!" Jonah exclaims. "I hate the Ninevites." But then he remembers how God freely forgives people who repent of their sin. Jonah concludes that his preaching mission might bring such repentance, so he runs away from

God's call. Nevertheless, God fashions a creative way to get him to Nineveh. By fish-transport, the unhappy Jonah gets to his ordained destination. After preaching his God-given message, Jonah suffers through the sincere penitence of the people. His dreaded enemies receive God's grace. He is not a happy man.

The two themes weave in and out, not just in the Old Testament but in the New Testament as well. The apostle Paul declares, "We have been set free from the curse of the law." But Jesus says "Not one jot or tittle of the law will pass away." Paul says, "We are justified by grace," but James says, "We are justified by works."

This intermingling of law and grace, works and faith, is not merely a matter of academic speculation. It is also an issue for living. How should we live? To err on the side of grace is to fall into sloppy living and God-embarrassing sin. To err on the side of law is to become legalistic, condemning, and rigid. The interface between law and grace especially affects our relationships with nonbelievers. Jesus loved sinners while still hating sin. Most of us, however, tend to do better in one area than the other. Either we indulge the sin that Jesus hates or we hate the sinner that Jesus loves.

To put it another way, when we sin and repent, we thank God for grace. When others sin, we call down God's judgment.

How does this all come together for us? How can children of the covenant, children of grace, make sense out of the law of God? To hear Paul, the covenant of law does have a certain splendor about it, but it cannot save us. Its words are written in stone. We need the words written in our hearts—such as is promised in the New Covenant. The Old Covenant results in condemnation and death, whereas the New Covenant brings righteousness and life. The Old restricts and tears down; the New sets free. The Old has a glory about it such that Moses has to cover his face with a veil, but the New allows us without a veil to behold the glory of God.

The Old Covenant of law does some good things. It gives us a glimpse of the holiness of God. It expresses God's desire to simplify our lives. It shows us that God is interested in community.

However, the key to understanding the Ten Commandments and the law demands one thing more. There is one prevailing understanding of the law that is essential to grasping its significance; one critical but overlooked fact that helps us weave together the themes of grace and works. It is to be found in the original story of the giving of the Ten Commandments to Moses.

The Law, the Dressmaker, and the Architect

It is true that God inscribed the law on stone tablets. Even that did not take place in a void. The commandments were given in the context of a long conversation between God and Moses. After being set free from Egypt and after crossing the sea, the whole nation of Israel went to the mountain of God, where Moses had had his personal, barefooted conversation with God. Upon their arrival, Moses ascended the mountain to meet with God. Before any mention of commandments, this is how the conversation began:

> Then Moses went up to God; the LORD called to him from the mountain, saying, "Thus you shall say to the house of Jacob, and tell the Israelites: You have seen what I did to the Egyptians, and how I bore you on eagles' wings and brought you to myself. Now therefore, if you obey my voice and keep my covenant, you shall be my treasured possession out of all the peoples. Indeed, the whole earth is mine, but you shall be for me a priestly kingdom and a holy nation. These are the words that you shall speak to the Israelites."
> (Ex. 19:3–6)

"I bore you on eagles' wings and brought you to myself." I am reminded of a friend who fell in love with a young Filipino woman while doing mission work there. For months he exchanged daily letters with her, nearly broke the bank making phone calls, negotiated with the immigration department, bought costly airline tickets, and to what end? He finally was able to fly his love across the sea, bringing his bride to himself.

These words of introduction by God are the words of greeting between a groom and bride. I "brought you to myself." That sounds like an old-fashioned romance. And "you shall be my treasured possession"—a precious keepsake; "a kingdom of priests"—ones who will introduce me to others; "a holy nation"—forsaking all others, I want you to be wholly mine. I love you so much I want you to become like me—holy.

In a sense, the giving of the law that would follow a few days later would be like purchasing a wedding dress. Now, to be sure, you could buy a wedding dress at any discount department store. At least in springtime, white dresses abound in such stores. A stingy parent would not mind the price. Maybe $79? On sale for $49? So what if it does not fit quite right. The dress is still white.

On the other hand, you could throw the budget to the wind and choose instead to go to a custom wedding dressmaker. You look through her portfolio of sample dresses. She takes all the measurements from every conceivable direction and angle, with a margin of error of just one or two millimeters. Then weeks later, when walking down the aisle on the special day the congregation's faces light up. "That dress," they whisper haltingly, "is her." It expresses your personality, your beauty, your joy. It discloses the love that is in your heart. The dress speaks, because the dress is you.

God says, I've brought you to myself to express myself through you. I want to put you on, make my abode with you, so I'm custom designing you to fit me. Now you are able to show forth the beauty, the grandeur, the glory that I am. Other people will see me in you.

Using a different analogy, God's intent is like purchasing a new home. When you buy a home, do you live in it just as it was when purchased? Or do you paint walls, hang new curtains, plant flowers and—if possible—put in new carpet? Don't you decorate the house to make it look like your home? Does it not become a way of expressing yourself to reflect who you are?

In fact, if you read the rest of that chapter in Moses' life (and the chapters that follow), God has a lot to say. God gives the law, the Ten Commandments, to shape the convictions and character of God's people. But that's not all. In fact, the law is just the introduction. God continues to talk and talk and talk. The primary topic is not law but interior decorating.

For chapter after chapter, God gives Moses detailed instruction for the construction and use of a house to be built for God. As writing styles go, it reads as engagingly as a set of blueprints. But the overall message is crucial. After centuries of estrangement, God is coming to the people to dwell among them. The house, known as a tabernacle (an old English word for tent), was to be constructed so that God could move into a sanctuary abode, akin to Eden or Mt. Sinai, in the midst of the people. God wanted to dwell with the people.

Unfortunately, God could not maintain direct contact with the people, as when they walked with God in the cool of the day. They could not come into God's room any more than they could go up God's mountain. God's holiness was too pure for sinners to endure. Such exposure would be like bathing in pure sulfuric acid.

God's room would have to be cordoned off from the people. So, inside a big tent there would be a smaller tent and inside that smaller tent an inner room. That was God's room, known as the Holy of Holies, or most holy place. Why? Because God wanted to be with the people—as close as possible but without destroying us or compromising God's character.

Moses conversed with God:

"Now if I have found favor in your sight, show me your ways, so that I may know you and find favor in your sight. Consider too that this nation is your people." [The Lord] said, "My presence will go with you, and I will give you rest." And [Moses] said to him, "If your presence will not go, do not carry us up from here. (Ex. 33:13–15)

The whole purpose of the commandments was to make a good fit for the relationship between God and us.

As Patrick D. Miller Jr., professor of Old Testament, has written: "In the commandments we encounter law that is personal. It does not assume an unidentified amorphous body, either as the originators or the recipients, but a relationship between two parties—no, more accurately, between God and 'you.'"

So the law and all its demands were not given to create a relationship with God but to enhance it. That could come only by way of God's coming to establish a relationship with us. But they are a way of shaping us to be as natural a fit as possible. They are given to help us become a fitting reflection and expression of God's personality through us.

Making a fit, making a home, making a dwelling place where God can comfortably dwell—that's what the law is about.

Ten Commands, Ten Promises

How can it work for us? As Jesus later would say, "If you love me, obey my commandments." As he made clear, obedience is ultimately an expression of love—not done under compulsion or fear (though those motivators can help in the extreme times) but out of a desire to please our Beloved. And under the New Covenant, the law becomes an inward work, a motivating principle planted in our hearts and minds. Thereby we are empowered to live in love and obedience, God bringing it about within us.

The experience of putting on the holiness of God hit home for Lisa, a fellow Bible school student. She wanted to please God in every way. But she had an overactive conscience. She felt guilty at every turn. However, when she returned from Christmas break during her freshman year, something was noticeably different about her. She glowed all over.

After standing together in line at the school cafeteria and after loading our hamburgers with ample supplies of ketchup and salt, we sat facing each other to eat our lunch. "Okay. Out with it," I demanded. "What's happened to you?"

Her grin widened. "Not much, really," she responded, "except that my best Christmas present came from God. He changed my life."

"What?"

"Well, I went to the Christmas Eve service with my parents. In my home church, we don't have a cross on the front wall. We have the Ten Commandments. You might say that our church gets a bit rigid with its regulations."

"So what happened?"

"Well, I'm afraid that my mind wandered a bit during the sermon. But as it did, I took another look at those commandments. Suddenly it occurred to me that I've been reading them all wrong.

I've seen them as the Ten Demands, prerequisites to pleasing God. But I realized that they're really not demands at all. They're promises! The Ten Promises: 'You shall have no false gods,' 'you shall not take my name in vain,' 'you shall not kill, steal, commit adultery, bear false witness.' With God working in me, writing God's law in my heart and mind, the commands are turned into promises.

"I cried through the whole rest of the sermon," she continued. "I now know that God is in me and is working in me to conform me to the image of Christ. I can relax knowing that God is doing it."

My hamburger tasted the best ever, even if it was cafeteria food. Her words opened my eyes, and I began to exude that same glow. A dwelling for God, an adornment for God's presence, a place of holiness, all accomplished by Holy Spirit's transforming power.

The apostle Paul says, "Put on the law of Christ," as an article of clothing—a wedding dress. Let the law adorn your outer being, he says, by taking it into your inner being.

When Moses presented all this to the people, they responded rather cautiously. When they saw the lightning, felt the thunder, heard the trumpet, and saw the mountain in smoke, they trembled with fear. They stayed at a distance and said to Moses, "Speak to us yourself and we will listen. But do not have God speak to us or we will die" (Ex. 20:19 NIV).

People have been saying that ever since. "Pastor, you talk to God. We'll keep our distance."

"Religious relative, you say grace. We'll keep our distance."

"Honey, you're more spiritual than I. You deal with those things, and I'll keep my distance."

God says, "I brought you to myself." God's desire is that we, in turn, give ourselves to God, that by way of such a union we sinners would say with humble thrill, "*Im anu el.* God is with us."

No, God's presence in us does not put a divine stamp of approval on our actions or our ideas. Certainly, many have claimed the name of *Christian* without a thread of genuineness and sincerity. But anyone who has sincerely bent the knee to declare, "Jesus is Lord" can say, "God is with me."

In turn and in time, as the law has its influence on our thoughts and activities, God can also say, "She expresses *me;* he shows forth *me,* and I am pleased."

God thrills to express God's self through us. God does so by showing forth moral purity and ethical integrity through us. God also paints and sings with divine creativity through our hands and voices. Sometimes in downright stupendous ways God's limitless creative power shows forth from us as Holy Spirit-Presence works within us.

Two of the first people ever to be instruments through which God trumpeted were rallied into service by the leader Moses. He helped them identify and use their spiritual gifts. Their names were Bezalel and Oholiab.

5

Spirit Filled—Spirit Skilled

*Y*ou can't raise the subject of Holy Spirit without somebody popping the question "What about spiritual gifts?"
What often follows is a heated discussion. Tempers flare.
Eventually, exasperated combatants agree to leave the subject alone. Too bad.

Without doubt, bestowing spiritual gifts is not the primary reason Holy Spirit would be given on Pentecost. The
long-awaited Spirit would descend upon the believers in
order to make contact, to bring the presence of God into the
lives of people. The spiritual gifting of people is merely a
by-product resulting from the entry of the all-powerful God
into a person's life.

On the other hand, spiritual gifting is a logical outcome
of such an indwelling. If the all-powerful God enters the
life of our weak humanity, doesn't it follow that some of
God's power might enter as well? If the all-loving Savior
went about doing good, healing the sick, and delivering the
oppressed, doesn't it follow that he would want to do the
same through us who are his body, the expression of his life
to the world?

Unfortunately, most discussions about the spiritual gifts
surround the quirky church found in ancient Corinth. As we
will see later, the Corinthians embraced the gospel with
enthusiasm, but soon turned it on its head. Their priorities
were skewed, and some of their behavior was shameful.
Accordingly, because the lengthiest teaching on the spiritual gifts is in the book of First Corinthians, it is not always

clear how to apply today the words of the apostle to that first-century church.

If we were to take a different tack by discussing the spiritual gifts on the basis of their first bestowal, we stand a chance of simplifying what later became so confused. In an attempt to aim for such clarity, let's go back to the days of Moses to meet the first two people ever filled with the Spirit and thereby gifted for ministry.

Meet Bezalel and Oholiab. Admittedly, in a book telling the stories of Adam and Eve, Abraham, Moses, David, Peter, and Paul, the names of Bezalel and Oholiab stand out like a paper airplane would at Los Angeles International Airport. However, their experience of God broke new ground in the Spirit's story. They were filled with Holy Spirit, and they were empowered as no one had been before.

The story of Bezalel (pronounced *bets*-uh-layl) and Oholiab (oh-*ho*-lee-ab) is a story about God's power gifting two average, everyday people. It is a story that elevates from the mundane to the miraculous. It is a story for you.

We meet Bezalel and Oholiab at the foot of Mount Sinai. Moses, having received the second edition of the Ten Commandments, has just instructed the people on the law of God as well as the plan of God to camp among the Israelites in a specially designed tent.

You can almost hear the people whispering to one another, "God is going to live with us? In a tent?" Of course, this could not be an ordinary tent. It would have to be designed with care, adhering to demanding specifications. It must be crafted out of the finest of materials and decorated with priceless furnishings.

A freewill offering was taken from the people. They brought everything from yarn to olive oil, from gem stones to animal hides. And of course they brought lots of silver and gold, appropriate for the heavenly King. But the people still pondered, how will this come about?

Moses addresses their question:

> Then Moses said to the Israelites: See, the LORD has called by name Bezalel son of Uri son of Hur, of the tribe of

Judah; he has filled him with divine spirit, with skill, intelligence, and knowledge in every kind of craft, to devise artistic designs, to work in gold, silver, and bronze, in cutting stones for setting, and in carving wood, in every kind of craft. And he has inspired him to teach, both him and Oholiab son of Ahisamach, of the tribe of Dan. He has filled them with skill to do every kind of work done by an artisan or by a designer or by an embroiderer in blue, purple, and crimson yarns, and in fine linen, or by a weaver—by any sort of artisan or skilled designer. Bezalel and Oholiab and every skillful one to whom the LORD has given skill and understanding to know how to do any work in the construction of the sanctuary shall work in accordance with all that the LORD has commanded. (Ex. 35:30–36:1)

Listening to this scripture and allowing it to be further developed by other passages on spiritual gifts can help us deduce several principles for their use.

Principle 1: Spiritual Gifts Always Bring Someone Closer to God

Before introducing Bezalel and Oholiab, God already made it clear what he intended to create. God wanted to dwell among the women and men of Israel and needed a carefully constructed dwelling in which to dwell. Toward that end God mobilizes Bezalel and Oholiab into service: to be architects, foremen, and lead craftsmen for the construction. And because of the holiness of God—which, if profaned, would turn against the people—the tent to be built must be done to fine-tuned specifications. Also, it must be created with an eye appeal worthy of its resident.

God wanted to be present with his people, so God gifted some of the people to connect him to them. Ever since then, all spiritual gifting has one essential goal in mind—bringing God to bear upon people's lives.

That is the starting point for all spiritual gifting. In the New Testament, especially in the book of First Corinthians, this is always the context within which spiritual gifts are mentioned.

God aims to be creating and re-creating, healing and revolutionizing people's lives. In fact, when filling one person with Holy Spirit, God immediately enlists that person into the creative process, particularly that of drawing others into being receptive to the Spirit's visitation.

Perhaps it is the loss of this perspective that has led to so much of the confusion over spiritual gifts. In Corinth, for example, the Christians there became so fascinated with speaking in tongues that they turned it into a litmus test for spirituality. They soon were dividing the church into two classes, the tongues-speakers and the nontongues-speakers, or as they variously put it, the spiritual ones and the carnal (literally, "fleshly") ones, or the approved ones and the unapproved (1 Cor. 11:19). The apostle Paul responded with harsh words, saying that the only litmus test for spirituality is that of love: those who unify the church are truly spiritual, and those who divide are carnal.

Like the confused Corinthians, some today are allowing spiritual gifts to be construed for the wrong purposes, whether as a litmus test or as a tool to entertain crowds or as a validating instrument for one's ministry. Those are not the reasons God gifts people. God gives spiritual gifts in order to extend God's own love through people. Using willing servants, God transforms them into conduits to pass on God's love.

This is made explicitly clear in the Greek word translated *charismata*, which conveys much more than its common English equivalent, spiritual gifts. The root, *charis,* means grace. The suffix, *mata,* means "portion of" or "expression of." In other words, what we have been calling a spiritual gift the scripture calls a concrete expression of grace. Some Christian circles have offered the alternate translation, gracelets; that is, the emphasis is not upon the gift but upon the goal—the extension of grace.

That's what the goal was in Corinth, and that's what the goal was at Mt. Sinai—with Bezalel and Oholiab. In Moses' day, God was determined to convey divine grace to the people. God's particular way of doing so was by moving near them into a house fit for the King of the universe. Holy Spirit filled and gifted two men to be the artisans and leaders to build such a house. They were gifted spiritually to bring God into people's lives.

Principle 2: Spiritual Gifts
Come in Limitless Varieties

If grace is God's unmerited favor—God's riches given us at Christ's expense—and if a spiritual gift is a means by which that favor is extended, then it follows that spiritual gifts would come in a variety of ways. Indeed, some of the spiritual gifts extend that grace in earth-shattering ways. When a prayer or touch of the hand instantaneously eradicates a cancer or opens blind eyes, nobody can deny that they have witnessed a miracle. To be sure, such miracles happened in Jesus' day and happen still today. In an age that has deified the natural processes and scientific laws, we become fascinated and, I'm afraid, excessively argumentative about the disruption of such laws. In simple reality, though, if God wants to extend healing grace to a dying woman or a deaf man, why hold back?

On the other hand, many miracles are overlooked because they happen in less nature-disrupting ways. For example, when someone has an unforeseen insight into a friend's troubles, and by sharing that insight the friend gains help, that too is a spiritual gift. You could call that a word of knowledge. Or when the neighbors are flooded out of their home and you roll up your pant legs to slosh around and mop up their carpets, that also is a spiritual gift. You could call that a gift of service. Or if someone's poverty leads you to donate generously, that would be a gift of giving. In other instances you might exercise gifts in evangelism or leadership or administration or music or compassion—demonstrated in any of its possible forms. Any means by which God's grace is extended is a charism, a gracelet.

In fact, the first gifts ever mentioned, those exercised by Bezalel and Oholiab, were those of artistic craft making and of leadership. In reality, there are many talented people using artistic skills in graceless ways. But when those talents or skills are exercised to give away God's grace, they become spiritual gifts. The scientists may not be offended and the crowds may not gather as they would for an international healing ministry meeting, but those efforts may be some of the most lasting means by which God's grace is given.

In actuality, spiritual gifts may be a matter of life status as well as one of ability. That is to say, one's station in life can be used as a means to extend God's grace just as can a special ability. The apostle Paul spoke of his singleness as a spiritual gift, allowing him greater mobility to spread the gospel. Then he acknowledged that some have that gift whereas others have "another" (1 Cor. 7:7). If singleness is the one gift, then what is the other? Why, it's marriage! Marriage offers the opportunity to show the adoring love of Jesus toward his bride and the adoring submission of Jesus to his Father. Marriage, singleness, employment, military service, club membership—many are the situations that can be used as a spiritual gift for the extending of God's grace.

Note that every extension of God's grace produces a miracle. It may turn the laws of science upside down and heal a sick child in the process. Then again, it may be overlooked for its simplicity. But when Christ's grace is given and when people find themselves drawn closer to God, that constitutes a miracle of earth-stopping proportions.

Perhaps it should be noted here that, although there are several lists of spiritual gifts in the New Testament, none of the lists aims to be comprehensive. When you compare the lists, you will notice that some overlap, others differ significantly, and still others simply have different points of emphasis. In fact, the lists are written in an impromptu style, offering examples of the limitless gracelets God gives us.

Principle 3: Spiritual Gifts
Are Discerned Along the Way

So how do you discern your spiritual gifts? Numerous diagnostic tools have been developed by church-growth experts, Christian psychologists, and conference speakers. No doubt, the surveys and diagnostic tests can help identify our specialized gifts.

However, most such surveys tend to assume a limited scope of possible gifts. Typically, they are based upon one of the gift lists (such as are found in Romans 12 or 1 Corinthians 12) or on an amassed total of the gifts specifically listed in scripture. Few take into account the almost unavoidable conclusion that the Bible's gift lists are just samples and that the number of possible spiritual gifts is limitless.

A more profitable and comprehensive way to discern spiritual gifts is by keeping an eye open to what God may do through you as you walk along on the way. A survey of spiritually gifted people in the Bible suggests this conclusion.

Actually, there are two ways Bible characters generally discern their spiritual gifts. Either the gifts are identified by a spiritual mentor when they are imparted, or they are discovered while responding to a need.

Bezalel and Oholiab were commissioned into work by the mentor of mentors, Moses himself. But did they receive their abilities then and there, or had they been doing artistic work before? We do not know. They may well have exhibited talent already. They may have demonstrated a readiness to serve God—even for many years. Then again, they may have been musicians by trade or shepherds by family assignment. Regardless of the background, the calling forth by Moses and the necessary infilling of the Spirit elevated their efforts from that of good art to godly ministry.

When Paul and Barnabas were sent out to do apostolic mission work, they went forth by way of the prayers of their Christian friends in Antioch. When Paul launched Timothy's ministry, he did so by prayerfully laying hands on his young friend and calling forth spiritual gifts for ministry. Others, such as Jesus' disciples, simply walked along the path with Jesus and learned his ways. They seized upon opportunities to pray for others, preach to others, and listen to others. In the process they discerned their own spiritual gifts.

To discern your spiritual gift, be a giving person. Lose yourself for the sake of others. You will find your gift along the way.

Principal 4: Spiritual Gifts Need to Be Exercised Decently and in Order

Finally, spiritual gifts function best when they work together in an orderly fashion. The problems of the ancient world are with us still. Then it was said, "The Jews seek a sign, the Greeks seek wisdom." Today we say, "I'll believe it when I see it." In fact, many a preacher has been drawn into portraying superficial displays of supernatural soothsaying just to satisfy an entertainment-hungry audience. The piqued emotions displayed in such gatherings have brought more shame upon the church than benefit.

The apostle urged the Corinthians in words that apply today: "All things should be done decently and in order" (1 Cor. 14:40). Paul's concern was that spiritual gifts be used not for one's own glory but as a means of service.

When Paul addresses the confusion surrounding spiritual gifts among the Corinthians, he writes them a lengthy corrective (chs. 12–14). He highlights the variety of gifts given by the one Spirit. He assures that no one's gifts are unimportant, and he scolds those who consider theirs to be more important than others'. He elevates the value of gifts that build up the community over those that merely build up one's self. He also gives some guidelines so that the gifts will be exercised with decency and order.

In the middle of the teaching he launches into one of the most quoted chapters in all the Bible. Used with the warmest sentiment in weddings, it is known as the love chapter. Ironically, his thoughts are not given with sentimental weddings in mind. They are conveyed as a stinging rebuke to those who elevate their glory—and spiritual gifting—above God's purposes.

> If I speak in the tongues of mortals and of angels, but do not have love, I am a noisy gong or a clanging cymbal. And if I have prophetic powers, and understand all mysteries and all knowledge, and if I have all faith, so as to remove mountains, but do not have love, I am nothing. If I give away all my possessions, and if I hand over my body so that I may boast, but do not have love, I gain nothing. (1 Cor. 13:1–3)

Paul's point is clear: God's grace is extended best by those who love most.

Also, "decency and order" necessitates working according to guidelines of decorum, good manners, and appropriateness. Paul told the Corinthians not to showcase their gifts of speaking in tongues in congregational gatherings. Rather, he said they should be used in one's private times of personal prayer. He did encourage the expression of prophecies for the congregation as means to build up the whole. But then again, he gave specific limits on the prophecies, lest they get out of hand (1 Corinthians 14).

So too, Bezalel and Oholiab were gifted not merely for artistry but for leadership as well. They were not given carte blanche to make whatever pleased them. They were handed specific instructions for the tasks at hand. Spiritual gifts function like the proverbial train; it works best when it stays on track.

So what can we conclude about spiritual gifts? Surely the indwelling Spirit, as given Oholiab and Bezalel, empowers the indwelt person with the power of God. Anyone in whom Holy Spirit abides is granted spiritual gifts as a concrete expression to others of the grace of God. However, we always need to keep in mind that those expressions may be simple or spectacular. If we are being used to extend God's grace, then they are gifts of the Spirit indeed.

Returning to the story of Bezalel and Oholiab, it is notable that their names tell a story. Oholiab means "father's tent." Constructing his Father's tent, in very fact, is what he was called to do—to build a tent for the holy Father.

Bezalel's name is a little more esoteric. His name means "in the shadow of God." What a wonderful name to give a child! Perhaps you have known a child who has followed closely in her mother's path. Neighbors comment, "She walks in her mother's shadow." That is a way of saying that she is the image or the reflection of her mother. Could it be that God preordained that Bezalel should be named as one who would craft and create with the eye and hand of the world's Creator?

One other thing is striking about the name Bezalel. If you were to go to Israel today and enroll in advanced artistic studies, the leading school in the field is called the Bezalel School of Art. What a legacy to study in a school named for the one gifted by Holy Spirit to create God's dwelling!

When their work was done, Bezalel and Oholiab assisted Moses in assembling and arranging the tent for God. The human task completed, they waited for God:

> Then the cloud covered the tent of meeting, and the glory of the LORD filled the tabernacle. Moses was not able to enter

the tent of meeting because the cloud settled upon it, and the glory of the LORD filled the tabernacle. Whenever the cloud was taken up from the tabernacle, the Israelites would set out on each stage of their journey; but if the cloud was not taken up, then they did not set out until the day that it was taken up. For the cloud of the LORD was on the tabernacle by day, and fire was in the cloud by night, before the eyes of all the house of Israel at each stage of their journey.

(Ex. 40:34–38)

Thus the program was complete. God gifted some in order to extend grace to all. So, too, does God gift you.

However, the tabernacle, constructed by the gifted Bezalel and Oholiab, provided not only the exodus wanderers a place of contact with God. Its legacy of communion with God was passed on from generation to generation. Even hundreds of years later, a few privileged individuals enjoyed the thrill of meeting God in a tent. Not only were they enabled to exercise their Spirit-empowered gifts. They learned that living the presence of the Spirit could bring intimate communion with the God of the tent. Nobody experienced such intimacy with greater intensity than did the shepherd-king named David.

6

Passion for the Presence

*P*hil Keaggy is my friend. I thought he considered me his friend, too, but I'm not so sure anymore.

Phil Keaggy is considered by many to be the most talented guitarist playing contemporary Christian music. Some even consider him the greatest guitarist playing any music. And yes, I once considered him my friend.

Back in the late 1970s, I was booking concerts for a local Christian concert series. The biggest event we ever organized was a series of six concerts stretched over five days. They featured the Phil Keaggy Band. I had bought and listened often to his every album. Now I had the thrill of sponsoring him in concert.

Four such concerts were presented as assemblies in local high schools and a college, with the two final concerts being sellouts at the largest nearby auditorium. Through the week, Phil stayed at my house. We had a blast!

My wife, Barbie, and I laughed our way through the week with Phil. At the local mall, we helped him pick out a new perfume fragrance to take home to his wife. He enlisted our help by spraying a separate puff of perfume on virtually every square of our arms. By the time we left the department store, an olfactory cloud preceded our physical presence by minutes!

Over meals we shared our personal histories. We prayed together. We felt close. By the end of the week, a banner week of evangelistic ministry and of growing in close fellowship, Phil parted with memorable words: "I really feel like we've become good friends. In fact, I'll always think of you as my New Jersey friends. Let's keep in touch."

While at seminary a few years later, I saw a poster advertising "In Concert: The Phil Keaggy Band." We had to go. Barbie and I headed to the Gordon College campus, packed into the auditorium with about 2,500 young adults, and sat through a three-hour exhibition of guitar mastery. As the crowd filed out and Barbie headed to the car to wait, I meandered backstage to say hello to my friend. A line of a dozen fans awaited autographs and handshakes. I was too proud to stand in such a line, so I just floated in the background until the others faded away. Finally, when just one person stood in line, I pulled myself forward to wait behind that last signature-seeker. When she turned to go, I looked at Phil, smiled, and said, "Great to see you, Phil! Super concert!"

"Thank you," he said, in a rather bland way considering that I was his friend.

Silence held us in check. His blank stare told me he didn't recognize me. It must have been that I was out of my home territory. I stuttered a stumbling staccato: "I'm Jack Haberer. From the Mustard Seed Coffeehouse. In New Jersey."

He nodded. "Hi." His voice sounded indifferent. Then he twisted his head and grabbed his chin. It struck a chord. "The Mustard Seed. That's right. Sure, we did some concerts there a couple of years ago."

"That's right," I breathed a sigh of relief. He remembered.

"The Mustard Seed. Now what's that guy's name?" He paused and pondered some more. "Oh, I remember. Ken. Ken Stuhr. Say 'hi' to Ken when you see him." He smiled and shook my hand. "Well, I better go help tear down equipment. Nice meeting you."

Dejection! What was it he had said two years ago? "I'll always think of you as my friends"? Then again, he had *also* said, "Let's keep in touch."

Funny, but it was a long time before I bought another Phil Keaggy album. The truth hurt. We weren't really friends. How could we be? Sure we had met, but we had not kept in touch.

Friendship with God strums a similar chord. It's one thing to meet God; it's another to really know God.

The presence of God brings with it a friendship with God. On a first-name basis, we can talk with One whose name is admired not only by music fans, but by billions of people the world over. But as in any human relationship, the quality of the relationship depends upon the frequency and the attentiveness of our communication.

No one in scripture learned this truth more colorfully than did King David. Old Testament scholar Walter Brueggemann says that David is the engine that drives the Hebrew imagination. There is good reason for that. When David sinned, he sinned boldly. When he repented, he repented remorsefully. He lived fast, judged foolishly, failed miserably, prospered lavishly, shared generously, complained vengefully, battled victoriously, and loved passionately. He was a shepherd, giant killer, harpist, fugitive, army general, adulterer, murderer, poet, songwriter, king. He lived out others' wildest fantasies, and he suffered others' darkest horrors.

In the midst of all that, David was paid life's highest compliment. He was called "a man with a heart for God." There is no greater thing that could be said of you: a man with a heart for God; a woman with a heart for God. What was it that made it possible? If David was indeed the engine that drove Israel's imagination, what was the fuel that powered his engine? What fed his passionate love for God? The fuel was nothing less than the presence of God.

Think back for a few moments to the story of God's tent in the wilderness. Commissioned by God, built by Bezalel and Oholiab, and assembled by Moses, this tent was God's house during the wilderness wanderings. This tent (also called *tabernacle*) had within it an inner room called the holy place, and in that room was yet another inner room called the Holy of Holies. That room was exclusively God's room, separated from the adjacent holy place by a thick woven curtain. Inside the Holy of Holies was a piece of furniture made famous in our day by the first Indiana Jones movie, *Raiders of the Lost Ark*. The ark of the covenant was a rectangular box the size of a footlocker (4 by $2\frac{1}{2}$ by $2\frac{1}{2}$ ft.), made of acacia wood and covered with gold. Inside were kept the tablets of the Ten Commandments, a pot of manna, and Aaron's rod. The gold lid had on each end a gold statue of a cherubim angel with outspread wings. This lid was known as the mercy seat.

What a perfect name for the lid! It was the seat on which sat the God of mercy. It was God's chair. Imagine! God's own chair in the midst of the people of Israel.

Over the generations that followed, the people were always careful to hallow the ark with its mercy seat. It could never be profaned. However, that all changed after Saul became their first king. At first he left the ark alone. Then in his wickedness he saw the ark as a tool to be used. On one occasion his soldiers went out into battle against the hated Philistines. They lost miserably. In fact, four thousand Israelite men perished in a day. Saul called his advisers into conference. Together they concurred that their only hope was to rally God's presence to the battle. Under the direction of Hophni and Phineas, the two sons of the high priest Eli, the ark of the covenant was taken from the Holy of Holies out to the field of battle.

At first glance, the soldiers shouted their approval. The ground shook from their exulting roar. The Philistines took note and began to panic. But in spite of their panic, they rallied and fought with reckless abandon. They decimated the Israelites. Within hours, thirty thousand Israelites perished. The battle was lost miserably. What is more, Hophni and Phineas were run through, and the ark was seized by the enemy. God's seat was captured by the pagan Philistines.

God was not happy with that. The Philistines put the ark by their statue-god-idol called Dagon, and the idol fell over the first night. They set it back up only to find it fallen over after the second night. After one more try, they found the idol broken into pieces. Soon the people broke out in tumors, their bodies covered with abscessing sores. A killing drought devastated their crops.

The Philistines gave the ark back to the Israelites. However, the Israelites were not sure what to do with it, so they left it in the northern territory in the home of Obed-Edom. In fact, they left it there for years on end.

Eventually Saul died, and David ascended the throne.

He called the whole nation together and said, "Let's go get the ark." They marched up to the Obed-Edom's to claim their seat of mercy. Through a series of deliberate steps, they brought it back to Jerusalem. David was so excited that he danced before the ark. His embarrassed wife, Michal, mocked and cursed him for such a show. The curse fell on her, however; she was struck barren.

As the biblical historian recounts the scene: "So all Israel brought up the ark of the covenant of the LORD with shouting, to the sound of the horn, trumpets, and cymbals, and made loud music on harps and lyres" (1 Chron. 15:28).

The Chronicler continues: "They brought in the ark of God, and set it inside the tent that David had pitched for it" (16:1a).

The Israelites no longer possessed the fancy tent of Moses' design with its inner Holy of Holies. All they had was a basic, single-room tent, an army-style tent. David placed the ark with the mercy seat in the tent. What he did next was remarkable. He went in. He directed his chief musician, Asaph, and the others to make music and prepare offerings for God. In fact, he commanded them to play nonstop, around the clock. But as they played their music outside, David went inside.

In times past, such contact had been expressly forbidden. No one could go into God's dwelling without being destroyed by the divine holiness. The lone exception, which was the chief priest's annual visit on the day of atonement (called today "Yom Kippur"), meant taking the ultimate risk. The high priest's friends would tie a rope around his ankle to drag him out in case God's holiness, finding the spiritual leader's integrity wanting, would destroy him.

Here, David took the ultimate license. He went into God's presence. He communed with God. In that special place, David got to know the Lord. He experienced the intimacy of God's presence, and in that presence he found strength, protection, blessing, joy. "In your presence there is fullness of joy," he wrote in one of his poems (Ps. 16:11).

There, too, David found forgiveness. After his illicit affair with Bathsheba and after plotting her husband's death, the child born to him took ill. The prophet Nathan confronted the king, threatening death upon the child. David went back to the palace (which overlooked this small tent). He went down into the cold, dank basement and stayed there around the clock for seven days and nights. He wept before God, praying for mercy to spare his son's life. After the son was pronounced dead, he went up into his room, washed, put ointment on his skin, and went next door to the tent of God. "He went into the house of the LORD, and worshiped" (2 Sam. 12:20). He went into God's presence and there found God's forgiveness.

David's experience of God's presence stands unique in the annals of the Old Testament era. Not only was he the first person since Moses to have open access to God, but that access would be given no one else until the birth of the Nazarene. There would be other intermittent contacts with God, but the Lord would largely be mediated to the people through the stone-cold institution of the Temple. In fact, David hoped to erect a temple in God's honor, but the Lord insisted that he was happy to remain in a tent. In time, Solomon, David's son, would erect the massive Temple. Upon its completion, its innermost room, the Holy of Holies, would be blessed with God's presence.

When Solomon had ended his prayer, fire came down from heaven and consumed the burnt offering and the sacrifices; and the glory of the LORD filled the temple. The priests could not enter the house of the LORD, because the glory of the LORD filled the LORD's house. When all the people of Israel saw the fire come down and the glory of the LORD on the temple, they bowed down on the pavement with their faces to the ground, and worshiped and gave thanks to the LORD, saying, "For he is good, for his steadfast love endures forever." (2 Chron. 7:1–3).

The people of Solomon's day reveled in the glory of the Presence in the Temple. But no one really enjoyed the Presence as had David.

Centuries later, the Savior would change the whole perspective on entering the Presence. No longer would Presence-contact entail going to a place, such as Mt. Zion (where Israel's temple was) or Mt. Gerizim (where the Samaritans had their temple). Rather, forgiveness now being an accomplished fact, we would no longer need to seek out the Presence. The Presence would seek us out. Holy Spirit would enter us. We would *become* God's dwelling place.

We need to learn from David's experience. When granted the Presence today, most of us do not fully appreciate what we have. The Spirit comes as a package deal: in the moment when a person welcomes Christ into his or her life, that person is justified by faith, forgiven of every past sin, bought out of the devil's control, adopted as God's child, incorporated into Christ's church body, granted an irrevocable ticket to heaven, and—as we are highlighting—filled with God's presence.

Frankly, that's too much to grasp. If I were God, I would dole it out piecemeal. But thankfully, I am not God. And thankfully, we have a person like David to help us both appreciate and learn how to live God's presence, especially with an eye toward nurturing our friendship with God.

An individual such as David can give us insight into living the Presence. He had a realistic appreciation for the Presence. He knew what a privilege he had—so much so, that he danced himself silly.

Have you ever known someone who does not like birthdays—someone who does not like all the attention and adulation that can come on such holidays? Like a wet washrag, such drab disinterest takes the fun out of such celebrations. Contrast such a person with the little child who can't sleep for three days in anticipation of the birthday. Visions of Lego worlds and video game mazes dance in the head. The exhilaration cannot be contained.

So it was for David going to that tent. Like the proverbial child in the candy shop or—in modern experience—a Russian visiting an American shopping mall, David was awestruck with having the Presence, Holy Spirit, with whom he could meet and converse.

We do well to learn from David—both his fervor for God's presence and his personal disciplines. Fortunately, we have a huge record of such things in the poetry he wrote, much of which is included in the book of Psalms. One of them, Psalm 27, outlines significant life-style patterns that he lived forth.

The first thing David did was to aim intently for God:

> One thing I asked of the LORD.
>   that will I seek after:
> to live in the house of the LORD
>   all the days of my life,

> to behold the beauty of the LORD,
> and to inquire in his temple.
>
> For he will hide me in his shelter
> in the day of trouble;
> he will conceal me under the cover of his tent;
> he will set me high on a rock.
>
> (Ps. 27:4–5)

It is a sad commentary on some churches today that the one person least thought about is God. We aim intently to reach the unchurched, to provide education for the children, to protect the morals of the teenagers, to watch out for the widows, to advocate for the marginalized, to feed the hungry, and to visit the sick. But what about God? We tend to get so preoccupied with growth, success, program, management, performance. David's one preoccupation was God. His one focus, his one desire was for God: to talk with God, to adore God, to love God, to listen to God.

If David could have had his way, he never would have left God's temple, the cloth tent. And although necessity called him away from the tent, he returned again and again. Even with the luxurious palace inviting him to its lush setting, he would have gladly traded the pomp for the simplicity of a relationship with God. With the palace came the reality that he was one of the most powerful men in the world. But what did that matter? The one thing he wanted was to know God.

David's love of such intimate knowing showed itself when in repentance he prayed:

> Create in me a clean heart, O God,
> and put a new and right spirit within me.
> Do not cast me away from your presence,
> and do not take your holy spirit from me.
>
> (Ps. 51:10, 11)

In praying to have his inner person made right, David expressed his need in two parallel statements: creating a clean heart and recreating a steadfast spirit. In pleading for continued contact, he also expressed his desire in two parallel statements: neither being cast away from God's presence nor enduring the disappearance of the Presence-Spirit. His greatest desire was to keep in touch with God, and that depended upon continued access to the Spirit in the tent.

Why is it that David's psalms overflow with intense adoration of God? First, he enjoyed the unique privilege of close contact. It is easy to take that for granted when the Presence goes with us wherever we are. We need to set a David-type of priority for our lives.

The Curé of Ars noticed a peasant farmer frequently kneeling in church for long periods without the slightest movement of his lips. He asked him, "What do you say to our Lord during these long visits?"

The farmer replied, "I say nothing to him. I look at him, and he looks at me."

That is enough. Just to behold God is enough.

Second, David threw himself wholly into God's care. Anybody who has spent any time in the Psalms has encountered the discomforting wrath of David toward his enemies. To hear him cry "Pluck out their eyes, tear off their arms and legs, destroy their children from the face of the earth" leaves many of us more pristine thinkers a bit squeamish. But there is a positive spin to such prayers. For one thing, they reveal that David's conversations with God were not drawn through some artificial filter of proper decorum. He was a real person with real feelings, and he felt free to communicate those feelings to the God he trusted. There was honesty in his conversations with God.

Moreover, in venting his desire for vengeance upon enemies, David was reaching to God to take care of his own anxieties. He threw himself into God's care. Accordingly, he testified:

> The LORD is my light and my salvation;
>   whom shall I fear?
> The LORD is the stronghold of my life;
>   of whom shall I be afraid?
>
> When evildoers assail me
>   to devour my flesh—
> my adversaries and foes—
>   they shall stumble and fall.

Though an army encamp against me,
my heart shall not fear;
though war rise up against me,
yet I will be confident.
(Ps. 27:1–3)

David realized that his security and hope lay in a force beyond his control. Though a military man, he knew that no army could ensure his security. He remembered well how King Saul had searched him out with an army and how God turned things around, delivering the king into David's merciful hands.

David knew enough to abandon into God's hands his own care.

Accordingly, we do well to cast ourselves into God's care. "Casting all your cares upon him for he cares for you."

Third, David allowed God to change his mind. Often as he prayed, his attitude would change. What started out as a prayer of vengeance would turn into a prayer for compassion. What began as a diatribe against his oppressors would be transformed into a prayer of thanks for God's abiding care.

When we allow worship and prayer to extend beyond a perfunctory "Praise the Lord" or "Amen," we may be surprised to behold its transforming power. The old-time Pentecostals like to use the expression "praying it through." I once asked one, "What do you mean by that? Are you trying to twist God's arm? Are you trying to convince God to agree with you?"

"Oh no," he responded. "We're praying as long as it takes to get us to agree with God." Praying through means praying us into God's will rather than praying God into ours.

As David prayed, he acknowledged that his troubles were a way in which God could change David's mindset and even transform his life. "Teach me your way, O LORD, and lead me on a level path because of my enemies" (v. 11). The process of persistent prayer allows us to be changed by it. Sometimes prayers are answered simply by the way the praying changes us.

Correspondingly, there is no functional product that results from praise and worship. Like watching a situation comedy on TV, worship is an activity that, when over, is over. When all is said and done, all has been said and nothing really has been done—or so it seems. But if you look below the surface, you realize that those who worshiped with sincere love and adoration for the Lord have emerged different from when they entered.

Fourth, David worshiped God for who God is: "I will offer in his tent sacrifices with shouts of joy; I will sing and make melody to the LORD" (v. 6b).

If anything stands out above all else in David's psalms, it is the intensity of his adoration of God. "Praise the Lord" rings out not as passing cliché but as an urgency, a necessity, a way of life. He sang, he danced, he made music, he recruited others to do so. His eye was not on the personal or political benefit. His eye was on giving God the honor that God is due.

Unlike brainy, rationalistic worship services, David sang lustily. Unlike purely emotional services, David knelt in rapt silence. When he did not feel like it, he did it anyway.

One of the more familiar Davidic quotes urges: "Bless the LORD, O my soul, and all that is within me, bless his holy name" (Ps. 103:1). That is a curious way to talk, for David is not talking to God or to the congregation. He is speaking to himself. "Self, bless the Lord. Everything that is in me, bless his holy name" would be an accurate, up-to-date translation of the verse. Apparently he experienced, as we all have, moments when he did not feel like worshiping God. But did he just drop out? Not at all. He spoke to himself; he commanded his innermost being to enter into worship. Why? Because God deserves to be worshiped.

In sum, David made the most of his incredible privilege. He was free to enter God's presence. He did so by exercising himself in two of the central Christian disciplines: worship and prayer. Moreover, he did not just act out his worship; he *was* a worshiper. There is a difference. Many people go to church and participate in its worship. Only a few people are worshipers. Only a few consider worship as a way of life, an essential part of who they are.

Are you a worshiper? No, I did not ask if you attend worship or sing in church or listen to sermons. I asked, "Are you a worshiper?" David was a worshiper. You can choose to be one, too.

Another notable Old Testament hero chose to be one. Although we know much less of his story and have recorded none of his songs, we do know that he worshiped God with a fervor like that of David. We also know that he learned to listen to God, to attend to the voice of God. In the process, he became a voice for God. He is remembered as the first of the great prophets. We know him as Elijah.

Before turning to Elijah, I should update you on my friend, Phil Keaggy. I ran into him a few years ago. He performed at my church as a part of a concert series booked by a local Christian radio station. Before the concert, I recounted to him my disenchanting story of our aborted friendship. I feigned a sadness that could evoke tears from a statue. With his lip quivering, he began to stutter through a sincere apology. Finally, when I could contain myself no longer, I slipped out a broad grin. "Of course you didn't remember me, Phil," I said. "I never kept in touch." Before long we were belly laughing together.

The concert proceeded as expected, and as usual, his musical artistry was incredible. After his concert, I waited in line with the other autograph seekers and attained his signature on his newest cassette tape. Then he smiled at me and said, "Jack Haberer from the Mustard Seed. That's right, isn't it?" I nodded. "I won't forget next time," he said.

"Sure you won't," I quipped. We both smiled a knowing smile.

A Deafening Silence

*A*braham had his conversations with God. Moses enjoyed his mountaintop experience of hearing God's voice in the burning bush. Bezalel got to build a beautiful tent for God, which in turn was visited by the glorious pillar of fire and smoke. David visited the mercy seat. But where does that leave you and me? We've never seen a burning bush that speaks to us. We've never danced before the ark of the covenant. And, unless you are one of the very rare exceptions, we have not heard God's voice—not in an audible way, at least. Where does that leave us?

When calling himself the good Shepherd, Jesus claimed that his sheep "know my voice" (John 10). That sounds great, but what about the times the sheep hear no voices? How are we to live the presence of the Spirit when we can't hear God?

Many Christians will testify that, at least at some times, they have known the leading of God in their lives. On one occasion or many, God has directed their paths in ways they have to call inspired. However, every Christian I have ever known has, at other times, despaired for the lack of that very leading. Periods—in some cases years—of silence hanging between one's self and God have had a haunting effect. What's wrong with me? Where have I gone wrong? Will I ever hear the voice of my Beloved again?

There is precedent for such silence. The three centuries preceding the birth of Jesus are known as the three hundred years of silence (also known as the Era of the Quenched Spirit). They were known for silence because those were years when there was no true prophet, no mouthpiece for God, among the people.

However, the silence supposedly ended with the advent of Jesus and the giving of Holy Spirit on Pentecost. Why then is silence the constant experience of countless Christians today?

Meet Elijah. Like the other prophets that followed him, he did not have to endure a life out of touch with the Spirit. By his baptism in Holy Spirit he was empowered to preach for God. In the process, he experienced one of the most stupendous strings of miracles a person has ever witnessed. Nevertheless, he also had to learn to listen to God in the silence.

It all started with one of those Monday-morning-after-the-revival-I-got-the-blues kind of days. Up until that blue day, Elijah had received miracles as part of his daily life. For example, when King Ahab married the pagan woman, Jezebel, Elijah prophesied a killing drought as punishment for the idolatry that followed. The blight hit just as predicted. As the sun grew hot and the land became parched, Elijah was led into the wilderness and was fed by ravens. When Elijah was taken in by an impoverished widow, God sustained them with flour that was never used up and oil that never ran dry. When the widow's son died, this prophet raised him from the dead.

Three years into the drought, Elijah challenged 450 false prophets of the idol to a duel, a miracle-making contest. He challenged them to call down fire from heaven. The prophets took up the challenge, singing and dancing incantations to their gods all day—with no results. Elijah taunted them. As the sun was setting, Elijah repaired an old altar consecrated to the Lord. He placed the bull on it, drenched everything in water (lest anybody doubt his ultimate result), prayed a short prayer, and woooosssshhh! A violent fire fell from heaven, incinerated the altar with the sacrifice, and dried up all the water. Just then a fabulous rain began to fall. The drought was over, and Elijah was a national hero.

Elijah lived a life of miracles. Then came Monday morning.

Ahab, watching it all, ran to Jezebel, and she launched into a fit of rage. She determined to do to Elijah what had been done to her treasured prophets (they had met an untimely demise). God's man of faith and power ran for his life. He headed south from

Israel to the wilderness. Despondent, he lay down beneath a shade tree and begged God to let him die. In despair he heard nothing but the deafening silence. He fell asleep. What happened next is critical for us to note. An angel came to Elijah and told him to get up and eat. There before him were a cake of bread and a jar of water. He ate. Still despondent, he lay down to sleep. The angel roused him again, fed him, and sent him on a journey into the wilderness.

Sometimes on the blue Monday mornings of life, we need to head into the wilderness. That may seem strange, but consider this. When Jesus was baptized by John and heard the loud declaration of the Father's love, where did he go next? To the wilderness. For forty days and nights. When the Israelites were led out of Egypt by incredible, miraculous means, where did they go next? Into the wilderness. For forty years.

In fact, what ensued for Elijah was a wilderness journey of his own. Almost as if we were watching Moses' exodus on a VCR tape running in reverse, we watch Elijah backtrack many incidents the wandering Israelites encountered. For example, he traveled forty days and nights. He arrived at the mountain of God and encountered the Lord there. While on the journey, an angel fed him bread and water, reminiscent of the manna that fell as dew and the water that was given from a rock.

However, some of Elijah's experiences differed from those of Moses. In particular, where Moses heard God loud and clear, Elijah heard silence.

When those moments of silence come for us, we need to head to the wilderness, too. It would be great if our faith journey offered us perpetual mountaintop views. However, it is obvious that every mountaintop is straddled by two valleys. Moreover, the mountaintops are mostly barren; the best fruit grows in the valleys.

Our modern world has told us that we can find spiritual rejuvenation simply by turning up the volume or increasing the speed. In an activity-driven and emotion-pumping era, we have learned to inebriate ourselves on adrenaline. Instead of coming to terms with the silence—better yet, to exult in the silence—many just drown it out. Rather, we need to do as did Elijah—eat for strength and retreat for silence.

Notice then where Elijah went. Retreating as commanded, he traveled forty days and nights to Horeb, the mountain of God. He knew God had been there before. Perhaps God would be there still. Elijah would return to his spiritual roots.

Years ago, when Barbie and I were engaged to be married, we committed to one of those long engagements, nearly fifteen-months' duration. We had originally planned to wait for graduation from our respective colleges. However, after about five months of enduring, we were growing impatient. We really did not want to wait, so we moved up our plans to Thanksgiving weekend. We would finish the school year as a married couple.

Hesitating just long enough to get a bit of counsel, we decided that Barbie should doublecheck our idea with our spiritual mentor, Paul Johansson, the dean of students at her school. Now Barbie had a way of twisting his arm to get anything she wanted, so we felt that such a meeting would be mostly a formality. He would give us his blessing.

When she presented our plan, his response was provocative: "Barbie, in years past, whom have you looked to in order to hear the will of God for your life?"

"Obviously," she responded, "my parents."

"Then you need to go talk to your parents."

What a terrible idea! We knew what they would say: "Finish school. Don't be in such a hurry. Marriage can wait a few months more." She did speak to them. Sure enough, they gave us all those parent-type responses.

We waited till graduation.

The dean's point was important. *Go back to where you have heard God before.* When silence is all we know and when guidance on what to do is unclear, we do well to go back to the mountains of God, the places where we know God has spoken before.

I have several preaching tapes given by spiritual mentors of my own; in times past, these tapes have spoken to the deepest places in my being. I listen to them again when the voice of God grows dim. I also have a few books that have touched me before; they provide a short retreat back to my spiritual roots. Sometimes a worship music tape will help. And there are places to which I can go and people with whom I can talk who help me regain my bearings—even parents.

Elijah knew enough to head to his spiritual roots—Horeb, the mountain of God. Upon his arrival, he went into a cave to spend the night. No sooner had he settled than he heard some noises. That had to be heartening, for Elijah knew that Moses had heard similarly. Moses had felt the mountain quake, and he knew: the God of all power was there. Moses had felt a mighty wind, and he knew: God the Spirit (which in Hebrew is the same word for wind) was there. He saw fire (God's most common form of self-disclosure) in a burning bush, and he knew: God was there.

The Lord said to Elijah (we don't know by what means God spoke): "Go out and stand on the mountain before the LORD, for the LORD is about to pass by" (1 Kings 19:11). Elijah emerged from the cave and looked around. A ferocious wind blew, rattling and rolling rocks around him. But Elijah realized, contrary to Moses' experience, that God was not in the wind. Then the ground shook with terrifying tremors, but God was not in the earthquake. Then there raged an explosive fire. But unlike as with Moses, God was not in the fire. Elijah was alone. God remained silent.

In that silent moment Elijah then heard God—in a different sort of way. What was it he heard? A still, small voice? Well, that is what most English Bible translations say. But in all actuality, most Hebrew scholars now tell us that this English expression is not entirely accurate. The most faithful translation for the Hebrew word is "sheer silence" (1 Kings 19:12 NRSV). A silence you can almost see through. Elijah heard sheer silence, and it was in that silence that he recognized God speaking.

Oh, it is thrilling to hear God in a loud, resonant voice or to see God in stupendous signs. But Elijah, who had had all that, now learned to hear God in a transparent silence.

We need to hear God in the *unimpressive* ways that God speaks, such as through the reading of scripture. Some of the Bible reads in quite unspectacular ways, but wisdom waits to be heard. It is not spewed forth by a mystical mountaintop guru. It is found in the direct reading of God's Word.

Speaking of wisdom, the greatest need of the church today is for this very gift. Yes, we need more courage, and we need more love, and we need more ethics. But we need most the exercise of wisdom, which often is heard and learned in silence. We need to learn to sit in silence and listen to the quiet calm of God's presence.

After Elijah recognized God's voice, the first words he heard spoken by God were in the form of a question: "What are you doing here, Elijah?" (1 Kings 19:9). If you think about it, that is a strange question for God to be asking, especially when you note that God asked him the same question twice. "What are you doing here, Elijah?" (v. 13). God knew why Elijah was there. God knows everything. Nevertheless, God wanted to hear it from Elijah. In so doing, God was saying something to Elijah: "If you will listen to your heart, you just might hear Me in the process."

Elijah responded, "I have been very zealous for the LORD, the God of hosts" (1 Kings 19:10, 14). As he heard himself speak, he knew who he was and what it was that drove him.

God often asks us similar questions. What is on your mind? What is important to you? What is your dream? Those thoughts and aspirations are important to God. God often uses them as conduits to redirect our life's paths. Such a communication tool is suggested in the psalmist's words: "Take delight in the LORD, and he will give you the desires of your heart" (Ps. 37:4). Would God want to give us anything that is not God's will? Of course not. But the psalmist suggests that if we make our first desire that of delighting in the Lord, then our other desires will be so shaped by God that they will, in time, become increasingly conformable to God's will. God will happily give such desires-of-the-heart to us as well.

Too often we are told to distrust our thoughts and feelings. Instead, as we are putting our first priority upon God and Christ's kingdom, to use Jesus' expression, God will often lead us by planting and nurturing the right desires within us, and God will see to it that "all the other things" will be added as well.

So, in order to hear God, Elijah learned to listen to his heart.

Finally, God gave a directive. It was not a monumental truth on which all other truths hang. It was just a simple directive, loosely paraphrased: "Go back the way you came, and get a few people to help you out." This summary statement is all God actually commands Elijah. What did God want of his prophet? God wanted him to go back to work, but to do so with the help of a few partnerships—those of Hazael the king, Jehu the prince, and Elisha the prophet. These men would help him understand God's will and accomplish it.

Time and again, it is in community with others that God speaks to us—through spiritual mentors, teachers and pastors, friends and confidants, spouses and, yes, even parents. Solicited and unsolicited, their words often bear in them the word of the Lord. Accordingly, a good rule of thumb is that any decision being made in secret is probably a wrong decision. God speaks to us in community and in counsel with others. So Elijah developed his partnerships.

We need to hear God in those moments of transparent silence. Accepting the quietness of the wilderness is a good starting point. Going back to spiritual roots and listening to trustworthy voices help. Maintaining a healthy skepticism of the fantastic, otherworldly means of communicating, and choosing in its place the obvious sources, like scripture, sensitize our hearing. Developing partnerships with others can help bring it all into focal clarity.

Elijah did just that. Then, once he had heard God in the silence, he returned to his people, taking up his ministry again.

As years went by, a small band of successor prophets built upon the legacy established by this wilderness wanderer. Hearing God and speaking for God, they followed the path paved by Elijah for centuries. One of the notables was a man named Daniel. He and three friends came to know this same God of mercy as one who has staying power. Daniel's attachment to his people would persist through even the most trying experiences. We turn now to his story as he too learned a bit about living the presence of the Spirit when the Spirit seems miles away.

When You Walk through the Night

*E*lijah discovered God's presence in the midst of silence. In fact, he discovered that it is in silence that God most often speaks. But how about God's presence in abject suffering? Where is God when people suffer? Consider, for example, the atrocities endured in wars.

On April 9, 1942, American and Filipino soldiers surrendered to Japan at the battle of Bataan. But then began the real horror. The Japanese captors poked their guns into their prisoners' backs and forced them to march for sixty miles to prison camp. Over that distance, one after another fell. One perished for lack of water; another was shot for requesting a drink. As they marched, they saw the dead bodies of their comrades. In all, ten thousand met their demise.

A number of the survivors gathered fifty years later to remember their horror. A newspaper reported, "Fifty years later the survivors carry mental and physical scars from their ordeal. The beatings still hurt. The hunger persists." Where was God in all of this?

Consider other kinds of suffering. One in every seven Americans was sexually abused as a child. One in every six Americans was physically abused as a child. One of every five Americans has been affected by alcoholism, either by the addiction itself or by being a family member of an alcoholic whose life-style is wreaking havoc on the rest of the family. Date rape has reached epidemic proportions, one out of every five women having reported such attacks, with many more never reporting them.

Add to those statistics the number of families that have

been affected by the AIDS epidemic, by cancer, by heart disease. Add the number of families driven from their homes by hurricanes, earthquakes, floods, and other natural disasters. Add the number of times disputes within congregations have driven people to quit the church, grinding to dust their own personal faith in Christ. Add it all together, and you have a lot of people asking, "Where is God in all of this?"

When you have suffered, have you not also asked, "Where is God?"

Space does not allow us to try to solve the philosophical problem of suffering, also known as the problem of evil. Many books have been written to explain how an all-loving, all-powerful God can allow suffering. Here, let us address the more personal, frightening question regarding how to deal with our own suffering: Where was God? Where was God when you were injured? Where was God when you loved—and lost? Whatever happened to the presence of Holy Spirit during your loved one's slow and painful death, or when you had to go to divorce court, or when you had to cope with scandal?

It would be convenient to avoid these questions. We could insulate ourselves, as many do, by saying, "I'll just count my blessings." Or we could confess our own complicity by conceding, "I just brought it upon myself." Or we can brush it off: "Let bygones be bygones." Then again, we can create a fantasy world of faith: "Oh, it's just a detour on the road to health and wealth." Or we can just deny it ever really happened.

Then again, we can do better. The book of Daniel introduces a few young men who also suffered. We usually hear their story told as one of courageous heroism: "If they could stand up for the faith under such duress, so should we." They did live forth such heroism. Moreover, the writer recounts their story with few expressions of sentimentality, no melodrama, no pleas for sympathy. However, if we get inside their story, we see another story.

We know them as Meshach, Shadrach, and Abednego—the three young men and the fiery furnace. Their ordeal did not begin in the furnace, however; it began as they huddled in the corner of their homes, hoping the war would end.

Childhood for these three young men had been a living hell.

They were hardly old enough to understand why, but they did understand what: their hometown of Jerusalem was a battleground. What they could not understand was that the foreign empire of Babylon had designs upon Jerusalem, because the Babylonians intended to control the travel routes both to Egypt and to Europe. Destroying the city would strategically eliminate a barrier to their international ambitions.

On one occasion, the battle had its most drastic effect on the boys. They were taken hostage. Captured by the Babylonians, they were carried in chains hundreds of desert miles to a new land they did not choose.

Upon arrival, King Nebuchadnezzar could not help but notice that these were good looking, strapping young men. So he drafted them to be administrators in his cabinet. They were pulled away from mother and dad—if their parents survived the blitz—and enlisted into the king's service.

There the king took away their names. History remembers them as Meshach, Shadrach, and Abednego, but those were not their given names. Mom and Dad named them Hananiah, Mishael, and Azariah—names that had on them the stamp of God. In fact, each name made mention of the name of God.

Do you remember the father and mother of Israel? Their given names actually were Abram and Sarai. But when God came into their lives, God added his name to theirs. Accordingly, Abram plus *Yah* became Abraham, and Sarai plus *Yah* became Sarah.

A similar dignity is shared by modern-day Muslims. When boxer Cassius Clay converted to the religion of Allah, as taught by Muhammad, he took the name Muhammad Ali.

In the same spirit, the parents of the three young men gave them names that included the two most common names for God, Yah and El. However, Nebuchadnezzar robbed them of their God-stamped names. Hananiah was renamed Shadrach, meaning, I am very fearful. Mishael was called Meshach, meaning, I am of little account. How would you like to grow up with that name? Azariah was changed to Abednego, the servant of Nebo, a Babylonian god. They were drafted into the service of the pagan nation.

Shortly after, the king erected a statue to his glory and ordered all people to give homage to the statue. The young men, upholding the Hebraic prohibition on idol worship, refused. Quickly they were accused, tried, and found guilty. In one horrifying moment, they were thrown into the fiery furnace.

Where was God in all of this? Nebuchadnezzar asked a similar question but in a taunting way: "What god will be able to rescue them from my hand?"

Where was God in all of this? Answer: God was there—with them.

Common talk today suggests that God disappears at such times. Maybe God was not at Auschwitz or Ethiopia. Perhaps God just abandoned the hostages in Iran or hurricane victims in South Florida. Maybe God doesn't show up in such places and at such times.

"I will never leave you nor forsake you," says Jesus. God *was* there, but God was not exempting them from human suffering either.

Being a person of faith does not mean we are exempted from suffering or insulated from the possibility of loss or grief or defeat. A fallen race and a fallen planet have produced a fallen and flawed life-style for all of us.

Where is God in all of this? You know the answer. God is right where he was when Jesus was the one suffering. God is right in the middle of it.

"Look," exclaimed Nebuchadnezzar. "I see four men walking around in the fire, unbound and unharmed. The fourth must be a god." No doubt, the pagan king little understood the theology of the Hebrews, and he could not comprehend the identity of the coming Messiah. But he could understand that divinity, visible for all eyes to see, was there with the three young men.

These young men understood that Immanuel was there. "God is with us!" Even in the nuclear heat, God was there.

When we suffer, God is with us, too; and God is with us in particular ways.

God with Us in Anticipation

God is with us insofar as Jesus has walked a similar road already. He learned obedience by the things he suffered. The prophet Isaiah saw it even before the fact:

> Surely he has borne our infirmities
>   and carried our diseases;
> yet we accounted him stricken,
>   struck down by God, and afflicted.
> But he was wounded for our transgressions,
>   crushed for our iniquities;
> upon him was the punishment that made us whole,
>   and by his bruises we are healed.
> All we like sheep have gone astray;
>   we have all turned to our own way,
> and the LORD has laid on him
>   the iniquity of us all.
>
> (Isa. 53:4–6)

Jesus has walked this road before. The pain of our loss he has felt. The struggle with disease he has wrestled. The questions of what is ahead he has asked. So we are exhorted to be "looking to Jesus the pioneer and perfecter of our faith, who for the sake of the joy that was set before him endured the cross, disregarding its shame, and has taken his seat at the right hand of the throne of God" (Heb. 12:2).

Jesus not only walked this road; he was right in the middle of it. What is more, he was with us, preparing us for a relationship with him.

God with Us Before
We Were with God

As you can tell, this whole discussion leads to the conclusion that the Spirit, having been received into that person's life in faith, is with every believer all the time. But what about those days before we welcomed the Spirit, those days before we believed?

The Spirit was with us then, too. Consider the fact that any person who accepts Christ into his or her life does not do so without help—God's help, that is. Receiving Christ does not come by our initiative but by his. Otherwise, what would be the point of baptizing an infant? When a child is baptized before proud parents and congregation, all those old enough to understand are claiming God's covenant promises for the child and are counting on God to provide the baby continued protection and care.

In fact, God makes good on those promises.

Can you recognize God's presence in your own life? Long before you believed and received Jesus into your life, Jesus had come to you to claim you and to woo you to himself. Holy Spirit won you over, like the hound of heaven, to make you God's own. You are never alone; you are never on your own.

God with Us by Faith

All the more, God is with you now by the indwelling Presence-Spirit. Consider the things Jesus said about Holy Spirit. He promised his disciples, "You know him, because he abides with you, and he will be in you" (John 14:17b). That is to say, Holy Spirit was present with the disciples because of Jesus' presence. However, the Spirit would soon be given them to live within them.

Consider how Jesus names the Spirit: "Comforter." The original Greek word used of this is *parakletos. Kaleo* means "to call," and *para* means "alongside." The Spirit is called alongside to be your advocate, your counselor, your helper. The Spirit is the One called alongside to work with you, to walk with you, to support you and carry you, to hold you together. The Spirit will be in you just as truly as the Spirit is near you now.

Think how significant this is when you are hurting, when what is going through your mind is, "Nobody understands me. Nobody cares. Nobody can help me now." Think what a difference it makes when you can say, "I am not alone. God is with me." Somehow, when we get clear in our minds the reality of God's presence and are no longer living by what we mistakenly perceive, our perspective changes radically.

When the three young men emerged from the furnace, the onlookers noted that the fire had not harmed their bodies, neither was their hair singed, nor was there even the smell of fire upon them. I, for one, have opened the oven too quickly and had my eyebrows singed. But not even the smell of fire was upon the young men.

I can think of a few people whose childhood was so singed that their brains had long stuffed the memories into the realm of the unknown. "I don't remember anything before I was six years old," said one. "I don't know anything about my childhood before high school," echoed another. On the other hand, some have memories they would love to forget.

I think of Thomas. I had had no idea of the torment he was enduring. One day, the torment became more than he could handle, so he pulled me aside and began to talk about himself. He was scared that I might be ashamed of him, but he also knew that he had to get it all off his chest. We agreed to pray through his confession.

I knew Thomas had recently endured an ugly divorce. What I had not known was the war that had been raging within him over his own sexuality. A practicing bisexual into his early adult years, marriage to a woman had seemed the right thing to do, but he found himself being drawn back to sexual promiscuity. Now he knew he could not live with himself anymore.

For hours on end, we prayed through his confession of sins past. In so doing, I invited him to visualize the Lord Jesus in the prayerful conversation. Repeatedly, he sensed the Lord saying to him, "I forgive you."

In time, he divulged that at the age of twelve, he had been seduced by a scout leader. Soon thereafter he was molested by an older teenage boy. How could he be blamed? When confessing the earliest sexual experiences, the Lord simply said, "It was not your doing. Someone else's sin injured you. But I was with you. And I shared your pain and shame with you. Let us together forgive the one who did this to you." It took a little doing at first, but Thomas realized that even in such horror, Jesus had not abandoned him. Though Christ had not shielded him from the pain, Jesus had suffered through the pain with him.

As we talked together, I shared that it seemed that his life had been like a huge mansion with a beautiful living room and kitchen. However, virtually every other room had been dirtied, damaged, and then sealed shut. As his past life was gradually recovered and resolved, it felt to him as though some of the rooms were opening up to him—cleaned and repaired. Finally, as we were closing one of our prayer times, his demeanor suddenly turned from shame to thrill. "I can see that house you were talking about," he said excitedly. "I just looked down this long hallway and suddenly every door and window flew open, a wind blew through, and all the dust, cobwebs, and filth were blown away. I'm free," he exclaimed, "I'm free."

When you look back to your past, perhaps you smell the fire. Or perhaps when you look back you find, as do many others, that you've lost your past. Your memory has been burned beyond recognition.

Popular writer Robert Fulghum has said, "You know what I want for Christmas? I want my childhood back. I know it doesn't make sense, but since when does Christmas make sense anyway? It's about a child of long ago and far away, and it's about the child of now in you and in me waiting behind the door of our hearts for something wonderful to happen."

Oh yes, to have that child back! Over the years, I have shared in such healing moments with other friends like Thomas. Holding the hands of Christ, they have been able to correct their memory—that is, to realize that they had never been abandoned, and that Jesus was ready, waiting to forgive their every sin. Time and again they have emerged with tears—sometimes weeping tears of pain, but mostly welling up with tears of relief. They say: "I've got my childhood back. I've got my freedom. I've got my self back. Jesus has healed me."

Some call it the healing of memories. I call it the correcting of memories. It's a matter of recognizing that Jesus was there all along. As the prophet Joel said, "I will repay you for the years that the swarming locust has eaten. . . . You shall eat in plenty and be satisfied, and praise the name of the LORD your God, who has dealt wondrously with you. And my people shall never again be put to shame" (Joel 2:25a, 26).

So it can be for you. There is no particular method—just take Jesus by the hand. Turn your face to the suffering and loss. Say, "Okay, Jesus, let's walk through it together for the future and for the past. And keep me aware that you are here with me to go through it."

Remember the story of Joseph, who was sold into Egyptian

slavery by his jealous older brothers. Years later, after he had proved himself faithful, he had risen to a position of prominence in Egypt. Famine had driven those brothers to Egypt to beg for food. When they finally realized who he was and in shame apologized to him, Joseph said simply, "You meant it for evil, but God meant it for good."

The same holds true in our lives. Others may well have intended evil for us, but God can reshape it for good. In the case of Shadrach, Meshach, and Abednego, the suffering and losses proved to be the door through which they would discover the Spirit's presence in a way never to be forgotten.

At the same time, a contemporary of the three young men was discovering another door through which the Presence intended to be known. The man was a prophet by the name of Ezekiel. The door opened, not to a fiery furnace but to a stony heart—one that had promise of becoming soft, malleable flesh. If only the Presence might roll away the stone and penetrate this newly chosen dwelling place!

A Heart of Gold?

*A*n old story is told about a guru from around the other side of the world. He had quite a following. His loyal disciples followed him wherever he went. Crowds would gather whenever he would speak, all wanting to hear what new insights he could offer on the meaning of life. When he had reached an old age, word spread that he was dying, possibly facing his last day.

So as he lay in his bed, his disciples gathered around, hoping to hear at least one last word of wisdom. His other followers gathered on the porch outside, and yet others came around, forming a line all the way down the street. Each one hoped to hear that one last word of wisdom.

As his breath became a little bit more labored, his disciples whispered to him, "Master, do you have a word of wisdom for us?"

The master propped himself up slightly and he whispered the words, "Life is like a river."

They whispered among themselves, "Life is like a river, life is like a river. . ."

Out on the porch the others begged to hear his wise words. They asked, "What did he say? What did he say?"

"Life is like a river," relayed the disciples. "Life is like a river."

The crowds out on the lawn and in the street pleaded to be let in on the secret, so the word passed on from one to the next. "Life is like a river" echoed down the street.

Finally the word reached the last fellow at the end of the

line. When he heard the guru's words, he frowned. Incredulous, he asked, "Life is like a river? What does he mean by that?"

Someone heard him and quickly echoed his doubt: "What does he mean by that?" Soon the retort was passed up the street, across the front lawn, through the porch, and on into the dying man's room. Finally one of his disciples queried, saying, "Master, what do you mean by 'life is like a river'?"

Again the guru pulled himself up a little bit, lifted his head off his pillow, and said, "Okay, so maybe life isn't like a river."

The so-called wisdom of gurus aside, how are you doing at keeping up with the current?

Call it what you want, but life *can* feel like a river. As the flow of the mighty river swelling its banks pulls you along, it can be awfully hard to keep your head above the swells. It is doubly hard to stay afloat when you recognize that those ferocious currents are largely going in the wrong direction. They are being driven by a world going awry.

When reading through the Old Testament, you can't help but feel like you are floating down white-water rapids on an inner tube, lacking even an oar to try to control your plunge into disaster. Israel's story is not for the fainthearted.

The People Impotent

Take, for example, Israel's place among the nations. In the days of Moses and Joshua, Israel could overcome any enemy. The very thought of the Israelites struck fear into the most ferocious of armies. Then came young David, who slew the giant with a single stone, putting the Philistine warriors to flight. And in Solomon's day, the nation reached a prominence and prestige unequaled in the world.

However, these high moments were woven through periods of pitiful decline. Not only did Moses and Joshua face a few humbling defeats along the way, but the years following brought national disintegration. Not having obeyed God's command to drive out all the Canaanites, the feudal tribe-states were easily subdued by marauding guerrillas.

Then, after reaching the heights of Solomon's day, the nation divided over competing kings' claims to the throne; the armies grew weak, and the nation was taken captive in stages by their enemies, the Assyrians and the Babylonians.

In short, they found themselves politically and emotionally impotent. It took little effort for the enemy to dismantle nearly everything that had defined them as the people of God.

The People Immoral

The white-water ride through their story leads not only to the feeling of paralysis; it leads also to the habits of wickedness.

Looking from our vantage point and considering the stories we have already contemplated, you can't help ask, "What could they have been thinking?"

Take, for example, the children of Israel gathered at Mt. Sinai. On the one hand, Moses was mediating the presence of God, being heralded by a fireworks-and-laserlight show that even today's pyrotechnic wizards could not re-create. What did the people do? They donated their finest gold to make a statue of a cow, so they could worship it. "What could they have been thinking?"

Take King David, the man after God's own heart. Electrifying as his tabernacle communion was, his eyes spied the naked beauty of one Bathsheba (the height of his royal balcony gave him a vantage point from which to peer into the ladies' public bathhouse). Not only did he send his servant to summon her to the palace for some frolicking. When he heard her news of the resulting pregnancy, he wove a plot to have her husband killed in battle. Blood was on his hands. "What could he have been thinking?"

Unfortunately, Moses' and David's experiences of failure-amid-glory were not unique. A cyclical pattern runs through the Old Testament stories, one of short-term revivals quickly followed by protracted seasons of immorality and rebellion against the law of God. "What could they have been thinking?"

The People Estranged

Israel's privilege of having contact with the Almighty was a privilege squandered. Not only had Adam and Eve chosen autonomy from God, producing the inevitable estrangement; their children and children's children, when offered a semblance of relationship with God, repeatedly ratified their parents' decision to reject the Creator. They kept God at arm's length.

Yes, they had their moments of renewal and revival, but inevitably their fervor would cool and their tenacity decay. Consider the time they recommitted themselves to be people of the law under King Josiah's leadership, only to revert to idolatry almost immediately after the king's death. Or consider when they returned from exile, determined to rebuild the Temple of the Lord, only to neglect it in favor of redecorating their homes.

Worst of all, the cyclical pattern of renewal and regression seems to have a downward pull. Each revival is a little shallower than the one before, and each sin that much more wicked and more damaging than before.

In reading such accounts you get the feeling that something is desperately wrong with all people. You see it played on Israel's stage, but it plays on every stage of every nation around the world and throughout history. Indeed, as you watch their story unfold, you catch a glimpse of yourself right there on stage with them. Their flaws mirror your own: faith bold enough to move mountains dynamited into a timidity that could not scale a pitcher's mound; zealous commitment to holiness subtly drawn into materialistic and lustful obsessions; courageous resolve to control your temper and tongue dissolving before the slightest provocation.

A Bold New Possibility

Into the dismay shouts a bold new idea. It comes from several voices, but one seems to shout the loudest.

Meet the prophet Ezekiel. As a young boy growing up in Jerusalem, he had seen the city sacked and men and women taken away to Babylon—among them Daniel and his friends. Some years later, in his teens, the armies came again to sack the city. This time they captured Ezekiel, along with ten thousand other Jerusalemites, and took them to the land of Babylon.

In one sense, the exile of the Jerusalemites was not terribly tortuous. They were allowed to settle in a city called Tel-abib.

They had their own homes. They were not subjected to shackles and chains. Nevertheless, they were refugees longing for a day when they might return to their beloved Jerusalem. They prayed and hoped for the day that God would set them free.

Numerous so-called prophets promised that God's favor would return them home imminently. However, one particular prophet, Jeremiah, sang a sad song, warning of even greater destruction to follow. Then Ezekiel, at around thirty years of age, was called into the prophetic ministry. God said, "I will put my word in your mouth, and you speak it."

Sure enough, Ezekiel sounded a lot like Jeremiah: "You haven't seen anything yet. Remember Jerusalem as we left it, because the next time you see it, it will be leveled to the ground. The temple will be desecrated, and then be destroyed. What's more," he said, "the destruction—both past and to come—will not occur due to the power of Babylon's armies but due to the evil of Israel's sins." The never-ending cycles of their powerlessness, their rebellion, and their estrangement would be their undoing.

Just as predicted, the word got to the exiles that destruction had come. Jerusalem again was sacked. It also was desecrated and then destroyed. The Temple was no more.

Soon Ezekiel was speaking a different word. With the destruction complete and the people despondent, he sensed a readiness in the people to confess their sinful self-destruction and to make things right with God. They seemed to recognize that something was radically wrong with them and that it would take a miraculous act of God to right the wrong. Although Ezekiel had been seeing them like a mother watching her children play in the mud—oblivious to the mess being made—they now were coming to the door asking how they could clean up their ways. They began to feel a chill in their inner beings. Their hearts had become stone-cold toward the warm, loving Creator. They knew that they needed God in their lives.

Ezekiel's preaching shifted from condemnation to comfort, from accusation to promise. As the Israelites cried out in despair, he spoke the word of hope. "A new day is coming," he said, "when God will cleanse us clean, will re-create our hearts, and will place his Spirit within us."

Sparkling Clean

"I will sprinkle clean water upon you, and you shall be clean" (Ezek. 36:25a). Have you ever washed yourself, but still didn't feel quite clean enough? I recall cleaning up after vandals unloaded three fire extinguishers of carbon dioxide in my church's educational wing. When we mopped the floors, they looked very shiny from the water, but once dry, there remained a thin film that still coated and dulled everything. We mopped and mopped, each time thinning that film but never eliminating it, never seeing the floor shine again. It took a harsh chemical stripper to finally cut through the film and allow a new bright wax to restore the original shine.

So it is with a lot of our efforts to clear our consciences. We give a peace offering, we make a sacrificial gesture toward someone, but we don't feel the chasm has been bridged. We go to great efforts in service to others and the needy, but our efforts don't quite clean us. The prophet said, the days are coming when you will be cleansed with clean water and you will be clean.

The people sat up and took notice. Really clean? They wanted that.

The New Heart

"A new heart I will give you . . . I will remove from your body the heart of stone and give you a heart of flesh" (Ezek. 36:26).

For the Israelite, the heart was not just the center of emotion as we tend to think of it. It was the center of everything. Whereas we might say, "use your head," meaning "think it through," they would say, "now think it through with your heart!" They would think with their heart and decide with their heart as well as feel with their heart.

According to the prophet, a day was coming when the whole inner person would be transformed from being stone-cold to being heart-warm.

It is not hard to see how the Israelites' hearts had become so stony. They had become but a reflection of their own misunderstandings of the law God had given them. As the apostle Paul would later elaborate, the law given them on stone tablets had led them to develop stony hearts. Not that the law was somehow evil; it was fitting for the people to try valiantly to follow its commands and avoid its taboos. However, they had given more attention to avoiding the appearance of evil than to being transformed on the inside into the image of God. What resulted was an *external prohibitory religiosity*—EPR, for short.

The Israelites promoted a style of living that avoided the slightest infraction of Sabbath laws, of kosher dietary rules, of overt immorality. All the while, their hearts were raging furnaces of lust, jealousy, envy, and bitterness. EPR was controlling them on the outside but petrifying them within.

Ezekiel envisioned a day when God would change it all on the inside. A heart of flesh—warm, soft, pliable—would replace their hearts of stone. A readiness to respond to the impulses of God's heart, a happy obedience to the Lord's will would be the rule and not the exception. Openhandedness toward needy people would be instinctual.

Really clean and a new heart! What more could they hope for? Ah, the best of all: the abiding presence of Holy Spirit in their lives: "I will put my spirit within you, and make you follow my statutes and be careful to observe my ordinances" (Ezek. 36:27).

The Indwelling Spirit

In one of the most dramatic experiences recorded in the Bible, Ezekiel was taken by God (whether by vision or actual travel we don't know) out to a valley wherein King Zedekiah and the Judeans had fought their last battle against the Babylonians. All that was left were the littered remains of dead soldiers' bones. God speaks to the prophet: "Mortal, can these bones live?" (Ezek. 37:3).

Ezekiel was tentative in his response. "O Lord GOD, you know" (v. 3).

God told the prophet to speak to the bones, saying, "I will cause breath [or spirit] to enter you, and you shall live" (v. 5). The bones started to rattle and began to come together. They grew skin and organs, but they still had no breath.

Then God commanded Ezekiel to speak to the winds: "Prophesy

to the breath [winds], prophesy, mortal, and say to the breath: Thus says the Lord GOD: Come from the four winds, O breath, and breathe upon these slain, that they may live" (v. 9). The reconstituted bodies suddenly inhaled a massive breath and came alive.

As this new army celebrated its rebirth, God explained to Ezekiel the significance of the experience. The bones, God said, are the exiled people of Judea and Israel. "I am going to open your graves, and bring you up from your graves, O my people; . . . I will make a covenant of peace with them; it shall be an everlasting covenant with them; and I will bless them and multiply them, and will set my sanctuary among them forevermore. My dwelling place shall be with them; and I will be their God, and they shall be my people. Then the nations shall know that I the LORD sanctify Israel, when my sanctuary is among them forevermore" (Ezek. 37:12b, 26–28).

In other words, Holy Spirit will come into their lives, they will be reborn, and they will live in and from and by the Spirit: "I will put my spirit within you, and make you follow my statutes and be careful to observe my ordinances. Then you shall live in the land that I gave to your ancestors; and you shall be my people, and I will be your God" (Ezek. 36:27–28). No longer mastered by external prohibitory religiosity, these people would someday be transformed from within by God living within by the presence of the Spirit. God's statutes, decrees, and plans would become the people's own instinctual action. In fact, the day is coming when "you will be my people and I will be your God."

Could it be that finally the decision of the first human couple would be overturned? That's what Ezekiel saw in the valley. Unfortunately, he never saw it in his lifetime. In fact, he never even made it back to Jerusalem. He died before the exiles were allowed to return to their homeland.

The people of Ezekiel's day did return to the land, but the rest of the dream remained just that—a dream—for many generations. In order for the constitutional change in humanity to occur, a radical new order of things would be required. A whole new framework of relationship with God would be needed. A new covenant would need to be enacted by God.

Accordingly, Ezekiel's mentor, the prophet Jeremiah, gave the people another glimpse of the coming day:

> The days are surely coming, says the LORD, when I will make a new covenant with the house of Israel and the house of Judah. It will not be like the covenant that I made with their ancestors when I took them by the hand to bring them out of the land of Egypt— a covenant that they broke, though I was their husband, says the LORD. But this is the covenant that I will make with the house of Israel after those days, says the LORD: I will put my law within them, and I will write it on their hearts; and I will be their God, and they shall be my people. (Jer. 31:31–33)

A change would come, but it would take more than a prophet to bring it about. God would have to do it. Perhaps God himself might come!

Alienation's Conquering Embrace

*C*hristmas. The very word propels children into merry dreams and sparkling visions. Its songs ring out in our memories, bringing cheer and hope. Then again, its demands cause our wallets to shrivel like prunes and our calendars to fill up like a Los Angeles freeway at rush hour. What's it all about?

Simply put, Christmas is God coming to be with us as a human. Frederick Buechner said it this way: "The claim that Christianity makes for Christmas is that at a particular time and place, God came to be with us himself."

While hearing all those Old Testament stories, we can't help but conclude, "These people desperately need a visit from God." The opportunity to know God was squandered, the power of God was lost, the holiness of God went unattained. In short, the people were lost. In fact, their privation went from bad to worse. It deteriorated so badly that, after the death of the prophet Malachi, they lost all contact with God. For three hundred years there was no one in the nation to speak for God. For three hundred years they endured the Era of the Quenched Spirit. They did not understand how to bridge the great divide, but those stories of God's visitations that their forebears had passed from earlier generations only intensified their bitter taste of alienation.

God felt that alienation, too. God had never been content with the chasm separating God's self from humanity. Yet, in spite of all the divine visitations made toward us through biblical history, none proved adequate.

No wonder Mary was "much perplexed" by the angel's appearance (Luke 1:29)! Hearing the announcement of her pregnancy, she sensed that a world-changing event was about to occur. "Far more than you know," we can now say to her. God was coming to earth—being conveyed to earth through *her.*

She had a lot of explaining to do. In a small, in-grown community such as hometown Nazareth, a pregnant teenager would provide great fodder for the town gossips. Being engaged to marry the gentlemanly Joseph meant that he too would have to endure the snide looks and behind-the-back whispering. He decided to cut off the relationship and send her out of town to protect both reputations.

His plans in place and bags packed, Joseph lay down to a long night's sleep. No doubt, his would be a restless sleep. Pangs of guilt mixed with disappointment over the prospect of sending her away. Their hopes and dreams had crashed. Worse yet, he did not know if he could really truly believe her report about this *divine* conception. After his tossing and turning quieted, his dreams went technicolor. One such dream caused him to bolt up and out of bed. "Immanuel," he whispered. "Immanuel."

As Joseph later told it, an angel appeared to him in a dream. "He addressed me by name. The angel said, 'Do not be afraid to take Mary home as your wife, because what is conceived in her is from the Holy Spirit.' "

Friends' instincts told them to be incredulous. His was a bizarre story. But they knew this man and young woman; their reputations for purity were impeccable. Could it be true?

He elaborated. "Remember what Isaiah wrote? 'The virgin will be with child and will give birth to a son, and they will call him Immanuel.' "

That word said all. Immanuel. A Hebrew word that was a combination of forms: *im,* being a preposition meaning "with"; *anu,* being the pronoun "us"; and *el,* being the name of God. *With-us-God.* With us is God. An incredible word! A stupendous name, yet a fitting name for this unique child! His birth would mark the inbreaking of God into human history.

Joseph wed his Mary, and as the nine months neared their completion, they traveled to Bethlehem, as was required by the

Roman census takers. There she brought forth her first son, Immanuel. His common name was Jesus.

No doubt it was a strange thing to live with God. In most respects Jesus was like other young children: needing to be fed and burped, learning to walk, accumulating a working vocabulary, shadowing his father the carpenter, going to synagogue. However, the few who knew his true identity recognized his exceptional feats: demonstrating an uncanny insight to the Hebrew scriptures, outworking even the most burly of men, holding forth an unrivaled attitude of generosity and compassion.

When baptized by John the Baptist, Jesus seemed to come out of hiding. Rather, he was pushed into the open. As he rose from the water, a pure white dove descended and lit upon him. As the people's attention piqued, out rang a heavenly voice, "This is my son in whom I am well pleased." Soon Jesus was teaching in synagogues, in streets, even in boats. As crowds gathered around, they could not help but feel closer to God. His presence elicited from many a faith they had not known before. In fact, miracles followed such faith. From others, life's confusions found new perspectives.

Those who knew Jesus best, the twelve disciples, recognized that his presence brought peace and calm where insecurity would normally control. However, there were those moments when Jesus would withdraw from them, such as the times he climbed a nearby hill to pray undistracted. In just a few minutes, the Twelve were squabbling over their rank order in Jesus' eyes.

One dark evening as Jesus and the disciples sailed across the Sea of Galilee, Jesus slept in the bow of the boat. A thunderous storm blew in, scaring the disciples even more than it was soaking them. What did they do? They panicked! They yelled instructions back and forth. They screamed as the lightning flashed all around. Then one reached over to wake Jesus. Seeing their frenzied activities, he shook his head in dismay, and with a sweeping wave of his hand toward the sky, he said, "Peace, be still." At once, the rain stopped, the wind quieted, and the waves disappeared.

Jesus' presence was wonderful to experience. But his absence—and even his sleep—left his best friends in disarray.

A Buzzword Fit for a King

It was in such contexts that Jesus taught about a coming day that would be better than the present. How, the disciples wondered, could it get any better than this? God is with us. Never before in the history of the world have people enjoyed the privilege of knowing God in the way we do. We've got a unique privilege. God really is with us!

The day was coming, however, said Jesus, when "I will ask the Father, and he will give you another Advocate, to be with you forever. This is the Spirit of truth, whom the world cannot receive, because it neither sees him nor knows him. You know him, because he abides with you, and he will be in you" (John 14:16–17). The Advocate (commonly translated, Counselor), Jesus was saying, is with you today on account of my being with you. However, the day is coming when the Advocate will be within you! Accordingly, wherever you go, the Advocate will go, too.

Jesus often spoke of that coming day by using a simple buzzword. A buzzword is a word that is understood by a select few and carries great meaning. Consider, for example, a freight car. As you sit in your automobile at a railroad trestle counting the train cars that go by, little do you know that in any one car may be the entire inventory of an antique shop a fortysomething woman is impatiently waiting to open, or a whole year's crop from a vegetable farmer, or the building materials to be used to construct a couple's first home. A buzzword is like that. It says a whole lot more than meets the eye, and only a few really understand its meaning.

There are a lot of buzzwords in use these days, both in the secular and religious context. For example, in the counseling world one hears of *dysfunctional families* or *twelve steps* or *codependency*. The business world has cycled through *MBO* and *TQM* and *excellence*. I like some of the buzzwords that come out of the world of meteorology, such as *positive differential vorticity advection*. They mean, "it's going to rain." Consider *conditional instability*, which means it may rain, or then again, maybe it won't rain; or the acronym *BICO*, which means "baby, it's cold outside." In the religious world, we have our own buzzwords, such as *Calvary, grace,* and *faith.*

One single buzzword hit the bull's eye of Jesus' preaching. That one buzzword summarized the bulk of his teaching. The one buzzword that was fit for the King of kings was the word *kingdom.*

Variously expressed as *kingdom of God* or *kingdom of heaven,* the kingdom theme pervaded every conversation. In fact, when Mark set out to tell the story of Jesus' life and ministry (being the first to write a Gospel account), the very first words Mark quotes out of Jesus' mouth speak of it: "The time is fulfilled, and the kingdom of God has come near; repent, and believe in the good news" (Mark 1:15).

In those days, such words could ignite a firestorm of anticipation. When Jesus spoke the word *kingdom,* the people's imaginations soared. In their minds' eyes they saw visions of their poverty being displaced by a royal wealth. They fantasized battle plans that finally would crush the oppressive Roman kingdom, allowing the new Jewish empirc to arise.

In actuality, what Jesus meant was something quite different. He kept the meaning for a few to really understand. He said, "To you has been given the secret of the kingdom of God, but for those outside, everything comes in parables; in order that 'they may indeed look, but not perceive, and may indeed listen, but not understand'" (Mark 4:11–12a).

Could it be that Jesus kept secrets? Absolutely. The day was coming when Immanuel's limited, temporal presence would be replaced by Holy Spirit's unlimited, abiding presence. The disciples would understand then what the kingdom is about. But until that time, only a few would be instructed about the kingdom's realities. Like a flight instructor teaching future pilots to fly by using classroom study and computer-generated flight simulators, Jesus was giving the disciples the needed advance training. Jesus' teaching of the kingdom was preparatory for the day when the kingdom anticipated would become the kingdom "that is within you."

Toward that end, Jesus told stories—parables—many of which painted a glimpse of the King and his kingdom. He compared God's kingship to that of a householder who requires his servants to give a reckoning for their work. One parable compared the kingdom to a farmer who sows seed and harvests his fields. Another related the kingdom to a judge who metes out justice. Others related to the owner of a vineyard, the owner of a fig tree, and a king who throws a great feast and then requires his guests to be properly dressed. This kingdom will have God as the sovereign over the people.

Jesus also taught that this kingdom would not be noted for its powerful armies and impressive institutions. No, he said, "My kingdom is not of this world." It is not one that you can go see and say, "Here it is or there it is." In fact, the kingdom would be demonstrated not by a realm of land and people, but by the actions of service. "You behold the kingdom," Jesus said, "when somebody gives a thirsty person a drink of cool water." In fact, the kingdom would not be limited to an exclusive group of people but must spread to all people. Like yeast put into a lump of dough, or light that drives out the darkness, the kingdom will open its doors to all who want to come in. In fact, he told the parable of the king's feast, where he says, "Go out into the highways and the byways and bring them all in and let them be a part of my banquet and feast and celebration."

Jesus' teaching was rather confusing. Though the kingdom buzzword germinated the people's fertile imaginations, they generally missed his point. What was the kingdom to be about? Amazingly, after Jesus died on the cross and rose again, and after he opened the scriptures to them amid his many postresurrection appearances, the people still did not understand. Their final words to him prior to his ascension summarized their confusion: "Lord, are you at this time going to restore the kingdom to Israel?"

At that point we would not fault Jesus if he simply had thrown up his hands in disgust. His disciples were clueless. Mercifully, he simply said, "It is not for you to know the times or periods that the Father has set. . . . But you will receive power when the Holy Spirit has come upon you" (Acts 1:7–8a).

In a few days hence the disciples would understand what they had never grasped before. The kingdom was something entirely different from what the most attentive students among them had perceived. Jesus' kingdom teaching talked about living the presence of the Spirit as would be experienced after the Pentecost outpouring following his ascension.

However, a few quick observations can be made about the secret of the kingdom.

First, the secret kingdom is just that—a secret. The biblical word for secret is *mysterion,* that is, mystery. It is observed not with the naked eye but with the enlightened eye. One of the central assumptions of the Bible's teaching is the fact that things are not as they appear. Although scientific observation sees things that are measurable and observable, the spiritual reality of God's existence stands behind every observed phenomenon. Accordingly, the kingdom of God is something that is pervasive—mixing and moving all around what we see and hear. And, to be sure, it is a reality more real than anything we can see or touch.

Second, citizenship in the kingdom brings attendant privileges. When, for example, the United States brought Puerto Rico and Guam into our nation as protectorates, their people gained citizenship, each economy gained favored status, and each island gained military protection. Correspondingly, when the King of the kingdom says to the citizens, "Be still and know that I am God," the King is promising to be their sovereign Defender and Provider.

Third, living in the kingdom also implies an obligation to the King. We need to acknowledge Jesus as our King who ought to be obeyed.

Finally, being in the kingdom means relating to other parts of the realm of the King's domain. Practically speaking, it requires us to enter into relationships of mutual support with other citizens in the kingdom—as they are gathered in communities known as local churches.

"Immanuel and his kingdom" means that God is with us and intends to remain with us.

The apostle John had a unique way of telling of the significance of Jesus' incarnation and promise. Of his birth, John wrote: "In the beginning was the Word, and the Word was with God, and the Word was God. . . . And the Word became flesh and lived [literally, 'tabernacled'] among us, and we have seen his glory, the glory as of a father's only son, full of grace and truth" (John

1:1, 14). The Word, that is, God the Communicator—became human flesh and tabernacled among the people, like the tent of Moses' day. Jesus was the living incarnation of the Holy of Holies, wherein the glory dwelt—just as did the pillar of fire and smoke, commonly known as the *Shekinah* glory.

Of Jesus' promise, John records the words of Jesus: "I will not leave you orphaned; I am coming to you. In a little while the world will no longer see me, but you will see me; because I live, you also will live. On that day you will know that I am in my Father, and you in me, and I in you" (John 14:18–20).

"The day is coming" Jesus said, "when I and the Father will be inseparably joined to you." Immanuel was with the people. But the best was yet to come. The kingdom's abiding presence soon would come. However, a chasm still remained. The Garden-of-Eden wall needed to be torn down. Jesus' mission was not yet complete. Strange as it might seem, in order to complete the mission, in order for him to become inextricably joined to us, Jesus would have to be violently shunned by his Father.

11

The Agony of Victory

*M*any writers have set out to study what makes Americans do the things they do and why. None has summarized America's brand of the human condition better than the granddaddy of all such studies. David Riesman's research in the 1950s led him to publish a book whose title says it all—*The Lonely Crowd.*

Loneliness is an American epidemic. Strangely, it is felt most pointedly when we are surrounded by crowds of people. Someone once related to me that she felt like she was constantly surrounded by sheets of cellophane wrap. She could see people around her, but she couldn't connect with them.

For many, that clear veil also forms an invisible ceiling, keeping an impenetrable barrier between them and God.

This barrier is not an American invention. Unlike store-bought cellophane, it is not a creation of modern technology. In fact, if we will allow our imaginations to think back to the faces surrounding Jesus, we can find lonely people also yearning to make contact. Some, such as lepers and the hemorrhaging woman, were trapped in sickened bodies. Their diseases cast them away from their communities. Some were caught by their misdeeds or their choice of disrespectable vocations; these were, for example, the tax collector, the adulterous woman, and the rich young man. Each one was cut off, and each one longed to break through the cellophane veil. With Jesus' help they did.

However, like Jesus' disciples, their contact was fleeting. They connected with Jesus, but once he went on his way, they returned to an existence of estrangement. More was *veil*

needed for Jesus to help people break through to a full relationship with God. Somehow the veil had to come down.

Whereas the inbreaking of Jesus into history as Immanuel brought God's presence to a few people, it took the killing of Jesus to bring God's presence to whoever would welcome him. Fortunately, his death—and the events of the subsequent fifty days—provided the missing link. It tore down the veil.

Humanly speaking, Jesus' death is rightly called "the great betrayal." One of his closest followers turned him over to venomous conspirators for the price of a few silver coins. Then by a series of illegal trials he was hurried through the system to bring about a quick execution.

On another level, Jesus' death could be called "the great reversal"—history's first innocent man being condemned to suffer the most heinous execution so that history's many guilty might be exonerated and live. On that level of understanding, the crucifixion resulted not from an evil plot but as the intended plan of a loving God. Realistically, Jesus had every opportunity to escape execution. Pilate would have been happy to deny him the opportunity of becoming another martyr, if only Jesus would deny some of the allegations against him. But he couldn't. He knew he had come for the expressed purpose of dying.

It happened something like this. Jesus' reputation was somewhat mixed. Those who knew him well recognized that he lived a life of impeccable integrity. He was honest, moral, pure, sincere, hardworking; the positive adjectives could go on and on. However, the people of power, both political and religious, saw him as a threat to their influence. They plotted together to bring about his demise.

All along, Jesus' integrity was serving several purposes. On the one hand, he was establishing the ultimate role model for people to follow. On the other hand, he was accomplishing what had never been done. He was living a sinless life. Without exception, he was resisting every form of temptation toward rebellion. Moreover, he was also living in constant contact with God his Father. Whatever his Father would want him to do, it would be done. By so doing, he was maintaining his right to live in relationship with God in heaven.

After the trials in kangaroo courts, this sinless Son of God was marched off to the hill on which he was to die. At nine in the morning, he was nailed to the cross and then hung out in the morning air for all to see. For three hours he agonized in pain. Then at noon the pain turned inward. He now faced the ultimate horror.

Hanging on the cross, Jesus experienced the most horrendous form of suffering he could imagine. He, the innocent one who had never known anything but the conscious presence of his Father, was suddenly cut off. The apostle Paul would later record, "For our sake he made him to be sin who knew no sin, so that in him we might become the righteousness of God" (2 Cor. 5:21). Jesus was suffering the same punishment experienced centuries before by Adam and Eve. He was ostracized, estranged from God. For three hours he was suspended in spiritual darkness as he bore in his own body every thought, word, or deed—every sin—ever committed by a human in the past, present, or future.

The spiritual darkness manifested itself physically when the noonday sun suddenly faded to black. Now the whole countryside convulsed in the horror of darkness. Then at three in the afternoon, Jesus cried out once again. "My God, my God, why have you forsaken me?" He was experiencing the unthinkable. Under the weight of human sin, he was being crushed. He cried out once more and breathed his last.

Across town, a shock ran through the religious establishment. They had been only too pleased to eliminate this insurrectionist, but now they weren't too sure. As three Gospel writers recorded (and a Jewish historian confirmed), the effect of Jesus' death was felt immediately, deep inside the massive Temple on the mount in the middle of Jerusalem. The writers mention it so simply and succinctly that, were it not repeated by three of Jesus' four biographers, it might be altogether overlooked: "And the curtain of the temple was torn in two, from top to bottom" (Mark 15:38).

What curtain? And of what significance? If you remember back to the days of Moses and his gifted craftsmen, Bezalel and Oholiab, you will remember how they built a tent of meeting to provide a place where they could meet God. That tent actually consisted of a small two-room tent built well within the perimeter of a large tent. The inner tent was called the holy place, and the back room of the tent was called the Holy of Holies. In there was kept the magnificent gold ark of the covenant. On its top were statues of the cherubim who had guarded the entrance to the Garden of Eden and now were assigned to guard God's tabernacle presence. Yes, this Holy of Holies was the room in which God dwelt. It could be entered by crawling under the veil separating it from the front room of the tent, but only once a year—on the day of atonement—and only by the high priest.

In time, that collection of tents within a tent was recrafted under King Solomon as a massive marble temple in the city of Jerusalem. Though destroyed by the Babylonians, it was rebuilt by Ezra and Nehemiah and later renovated by King Herod in the years prior to and during Jesus' days as Immanuel.

The Temple stood as a constant reminder both of Israel's greatest privilege and of Israel's greatest frustration. God dwelling in the heart of their capital city? What privilege! But God cut off from direct contact? What frustration! So near, yet so far.

As Jesus drew his last breath, everything changed. The Temple veil dividing the Holy of Holies from the outside world was torn from top to bottom. And what then? God got out. The veil of separation had been necessitated by the guilt of human sin. Now, however, Jesus had borne that guilt on the cross, thereby canceling its claim upon us. God no longer needed to stay cordoned off from people. God's holiness would not automatically blister and burn their humanity, nor would they automatically taint God's holiness. God could entertain the possibility of direct contact with people.

Not all was solved, however. Jesus lay dead in the tomb, defeated by the ordeal. Yet that also changed when on the third day he rose from the dead, laying claim to the victory his abiding relationship with the Father had earned. By so doing, he vanquished forever the power of death, the final end of our estrangement from God.

Over the next forty days Jesus made contact with the unsuspecting disciples in unexpected places. Finally, as his time came to go, he promised to them the coming Spirit-Presence, and then, with eyes lifted upward, he ascended aloft to heaven.

The apostles, along with the larger gathering of followers—
120 altogether—immediately formed a habit of praying together
daily. Jesus' death had left them in despair. They had returned to
fishing. Now his ascension also took him away from them.
Though they went into hiding, they sensed there must be something more. So they prayed, and they prayed more. For ten days
they prayed at every opportunity. All the while their frail faith
was buoyed by his orders to wait in Jerusalem "for the promise
of the Father. 'This,' he said, 'is what you have heard from me;
for John baptized with water, but you will be baptized with the
Holy Spirit not many days from now'" (Acts 1:4b–5).

After ten days of prayer with no results, their heads were
hanging. Then came the Hebrew holy day of Pentecost. What
would good Jews do on Pentecost? They would head to the Temple. They dragged their diminished spirits to services only to hear
again those scriptures quoted every year on this festival day.
They heard of the original call to the Feast of Weeks, as it was
properly titled (Pentecost came into being as a name because the
word means "fifty days," and the feast fell on the fiftieth day after
the holy day of Passover). They heard the priest read from the
holy book about the giving of the law amid the cloud-covered
mountain, where God had dwelt in fire.

Oh, how they longed for a day like that day! How they longed
for the place that would be a dwelling for God!

Then another priest took out the scroll of Ezekiel and recounted
the prophet's first vision: "As I looked, a stormy wind came out
of the north: a great cloud with brightness around it and fire
flashing forth continually, and in the middle of the fire, something like gleaming amber. . . . This was the appearance of the
likeness of the glory of the LORD. When I saw it, I fell on my face,
and I heard the voice of someone speaking" (Ezek. 1:4, 28b). Ah,
the vision of glory! Ezekiel got to see it. "Why can't we?" they
pined.

Then came the readings from the Psalms, including King
David's retelling of God's triumphal march in the ark of the
covenant from Mt. Sinai to Jerusalem's Mt. Zion: "O God, when
you went out before your people, when you marched through the
wilderness, the earth quaked, the heavens poured down rain at the

presence of God, the God of Sinai, at the presence of God, the God of Israel. . . . Why do you look with envy, O many-peaked mountain, at the mount that God desired for his abode, where the LORD will reside forever? . . . [T]he Lord came from Sinai into the holy place. . . . Awesome is God in his sanctuary, the God of Israel; he gives power and strength to his people. Blessed be God!" (Ps. 68:7–8, 16–17, 35).

If these upper room prayer warriors had had any idea of what was coming, they would have been jumping out of their skins. There would have been remembrances of God thundering on Mt. Sinai, prospects of the Spirit among them, visions of the sanctuary of God. But it was a dispirited and downtrodden group that returned to its praying place.

They walked back, speaking little. They wanted to be faithful, staying in Jerusalem until filled with the Spirit—whatever that meant. But they were growing weary.

Back in the room, they again set their hearts to prayer. It was very quiet at first—almost deafeningly so—but gradually hope was born in their midst. They began to pray for a new beginning, for the kingdom to be restored to Israel once and for all. For the first time since seeing Jesus' ascension, they sensed that their prayers also were ascending to heaven. An air of expectancy was taking hold.

Suddenly they heard the sound of a powerful wind—a tornado's roar. But it was coming down from the sky—from heaven. The sound filled the room. Immediately they saw what appeared to be a huge flame in the room. Then, like seed spread over a field, the flame divided and became as tiny flames over each individual. Before the disciples had a chance to think, they were shouting praises to God. What magnificent praises! Their voices were so loud that they were slow to realize that they were not speaking in their own tongues but in new languages.

Knowing that an event of eternal consequence was happening, they rushed back to the Temple, making no effort to suppress their overwhelming joy. As they walked, crowds gathered around them wondering and scoffing.

As they walked, Peter's mind raced: fire; wind; new tongues; the morning's scripture readings; Mt. Sinai covered with smoke because the Lord descended upon it in fire; "I looked and saw a windstorm"; the Spirit; fire; the appearance of the likeness of the glory of the Lord! Peter remembered "Immanuel tabernacling" among them; receiving Holy Spirit; the coming Comforter; the curtain torn in two. Aha! Shekinah! Dwelling place! Everlasting covenant! New spirit and heart! The Spirit poured upon us from on high! This is it!

Upon arrival at the Temple, Peter was bursting with excitement: "Let this be known to you, and listen to what I say. Indeed, these are not drunk, as you suppose, for it is only nine o'clock in the morning. No, this is what was spoken through the prophet Joel: 'In the last days it will be, God declares, that I will pour out my Spirit upon all flesh. . . . Then everyone who calls on the name of the Lord shall be saved'" (Acts 2:14–17a, 21).

Holy Spirit presence was now among and within men and women. Holy Spirit was dwelling in "everyone who called."

Admittedly, some license is taken when trying to read the minds of people who lived centuries ago. Peter's train of thought may have taken some different turns than those outlined above. What is clear, however, is that he and the apostles finally realized why Jesus had come. Not only had he brought a teaching mission. Not only had he come to die for our sins. Not only had he risen to overcome death. Ultimately, he came to destroy once and for all that veil separating people from God and to fill them with the presence of God. His central purpose was to put people into a direct, conversational, abiding, indwelling relationship with God as Father, Son, and Holy Spirit.

The imagery of the Temple, the natural phenomena of fire and wind, the miraculous gift of new languages were all forms of picture language to help the people see that the new day had dawned. The hope and expectation held in the breast of every faithful believer from Abraham to Zechariah had now been fulfilled.

What then about that cellophane veil? What about all the loneliness? In its essence, loneliness does not mean lack of friends; it means lack of love in the heart. That love has to come not from a changeable source, like human friends, but from the One that is consistently loving. True love and, correspondingly, true friendship come from God.

Prior to embracing Jesus Christ as my Savior and Lord, I had lots of friends. I had played my odds right and, at age fourteen, had finagled my way into five different crowds of friends. However, when at age fifteen I said "Yes" to Jesus, most of those friends said "No" to me. In a matter of two weeks I lost virtually all my friends. However, I did have the privilege of leading one of those friends to Christ. On a particular Friday evening that spring, I was walking across a field to go to my friend John's house. The strangest sensation crossed my mind. I noticed I had a light skip in my gait. I thought to myself, how can this be? Here it is a Friday night, and I have only one friend I can possibly get together with. Yet I feel happy—really happy.

As quickly as I articulated the question, I expressed the answer: "I've got the one Friend who will never stop being my Friend." No matter what the reason, no matter how I fail him. I have the Friend that will never stop being my Friend. And I've got my other friend, John, as a bonus.

I was content.

The cellophane veil had been torn down, and my heart had been filled. As it was for Peter and his friends, so it was for me. Jesus who had come on Christmas morning, had now come again—not to fill a mother's open arms but to fill, by his Spirit, my open heart.

No one had told me, however, that his gracious invasion would not stop at turning my life upside down. I soon found out that it also turned me inside out. Moreover, God's presence within me began to show *through* me. The glow on my face, the transformation of my attitudes, a newfound spontaneous generosity surprised nobody more than it did me—except my parents and siblings who well knew my other side. God was at work within me. And when those former friends mockingly called me "Saint Jack," I felt a bit embarrassed; but unbeknownst to me, God was saying, "That's what I call him, too!"

Sainted Sinners

Ah, the joy of knowing Christ! Never to be alone, never to be without his presence within us—that is joy unspeakable! And to think that this gift fulfills the hope of the ages, the reconciliation of which men and women have dreamed through the centuries. Now in Jesus Christ it is available to anyone who will believe.

Some questions still hang in the air, however. Probably chiefest of all is the simple query, "How shall we then live?" If the Spirit of God is resident within our hearts, what difference does that make? "How shall we then live?"

To hear some reports, one would think that living the presence of the Spirit is not only joy unspeakable but also happiness without interruption. Personal testimonies to the power of God and the experience of God's holiness sound wonderful indeed. However, when you get inside the homes of those shouting so loud to God's glory, you generally find less than glory. Their homes—like yours—possess a flaw or two.

On the other hand, one can get cynical at the appearance of Christians whose personal habits mirror those of their nonbelieving counterparts. Does knowing the presence of God make a difference?

We have to begin with knowing who we are.

Knowing Who You Are

Meet the man named Paul. A scholarly Jew and an enthusiastic persecutor of those claiming that Jesus was Messiah,

Paul was startled by a vision of Jesus and quickly converted to the faith. Before long he was preaching to Jews and non-Jews alike about Jesus. He was inviting them to receive God's salvation given by grace alone and received through faith. Soon churches were being birthed through his midwifery. Beginning around the year A.D. 45 and continuing for about twenty years, he wrote letters to those churches and to some individual followers, usually with the intent of correcting some misconception or misbehavior. Recognized as uniquely inspired by Holy Spirit, those letters comprise a large part of the New Testament.

One of the curiosities of the letters of the apostle Paul is that, in one breath, he scolds Christians as if they were despicable sinners, and, in the next breath, he glibly calls them saints.

What comes to mind when you hear the term *saint?* Perhaps you think of Saint Peter or Saint John. Perhaps Saint Augustine and Saint Francis of Assisi come to mind. Generally speaking, most of us think of saints as exceptional people who lived lives of unimpeachable holiness.

That thought is only half right. The word *saint,* as used in the biblical languages, means literally, "a holy person." In fact, the words, *holy, holiness, saint,* and *saintly* are various English language forms for one basic Greek word, *hagios.* However, saints are not necessarily unimpeachable in their holiness.

The apostle Paul addressed most of his letters to the "saints" in such-and-such city (see Rom. 1:7; 1 Cor. 1:2; 2 Cor. 1:2; Eph. 1:1, etc.). However, in most cases he then proceeded to blast the recipients as if they were wicked sinners. Is that not a contradiction? It certainly is, if one is looking from only one point of view. Sinners sin and holy people do not sin—plain and simple.

It is not quite that simple. The apostle well knew that there is a big difference between status and practice. In most of life's functions, we have to earn our status by our practice. That is to say, with sufficient lessons and many hours of rehearsing, one can call oneself a violinist. Or with years of education and internship, not to mention sleepless nights, one can claim the title of teacher. Status follows practice. However, there are exceptions. For example, one becomes a prince by royal birth, not by effort. A newborn child is bestowed a name, a family parentage, and national citizenship without having done anything to earn them. In reality, such status precedes and defines the practice that is to follow.

When a person embraces Jesus Christ as Savior and Lord, she or he is granted an incredible status. He finds that he is an adopted child, having been taken in by a heavenly Father. She discovers that she is forgiven of all wrongs and, like an acquitted criminal, is released from her own emotional incarceration. He learns that he has been redeemed, that is, purchased as God's possession. She realizes that she has been included in a preexisting covenant agreement between God and his own royal subjects that was instituted by the shedding of Jesus' blood. Each believer is accorded the status of a holy person, a saint, whether the believer comprehends it or not.

What the apostle is stating is that all believers, having been forgiven of their sins and filled with Holy Spirit, are granted the incredible status of being holy before God, totally complete and acceptable to God. This status in essence bears out the meaning of the central word for Christian beliefs, namely, "grace." Often taught in Sunday school by the acronym God's-Riches-At-Christ's-Expense, grace means, simply, unmerited favor. To receive grace is to receive God's favor without having earned it. To live grace is to continue to experience that favor without earning it. It comes free.

This status reflects a very healthy psychology of human behavior. People tend to live up to whatever reputation they are given. They live out their status. Tell a child that he is a liar, and he will tell you lies. Tell an adult that she is a gossip, and she will gossip. Make blanket declarations about a group of people, and they will live up to their reputation. Whether good or bad, we instinctively tend to do as we are told we are. We fulfill our status.

The proclamation of the apostle Paul is that we are completely accepted, completely loved, and completely complete in Jesus Christ—no matter what the external evidence says.

Becoming Who We Are

No doubt, that external evidence could afford to show some improvement. Fortunately, when holiness invades sinfulness, that sinfulness almost inevitably will be changed by the foreign, positive influence. However, for that to be actualized in our lives, we need to become participants, not just passive recipients.

The first thing we need do is to acknowledge who we are. For us to become, in practice, the people we could be, we need to begin by acknowledging that we are complete in Christ. If we join the ranks of wretches groveling in the dust in utter shame before God, we will never show forth the privilege of being the dwelling of God. The Christian can stand with head held high and say: "I am loved beyond measure. I am an object of God's adoration. I am a home in which God dwells by the Spirit."

Second, we need to recognize that God fully intends to reshape our thinking and behavior according to the same standards God set down when giving the commandments to Moses. God has found a people who, by reason of Jesus' death and resurrection, are a fit dwelling for his presence. However, God still aims to make that a perfect fit. Toward that end, the entry of the Spirit into our lives also has brought the corresponding deposit of God's laws.

Do you remember the prophecies of Ezekiel and Jeremiah, how God would begin a whole new order of things, and the mark of that order would be a transformation of the human heart and the writing of the laws of God onto that heart? Well, the inner transformation begins when Holy Spirit enters the heart of the new believer. The impartation of Holy Spirit into our lives allows the Holy One to work within us to re-form our desires, to purify our motivations, to reprogram our habits, to restructure our priorities, and to refocus our aspirations.

The Bible uses the verb *sanctify* (from the word *saint*) to express the process of purification: "May the God of peace himself sanctify you entirely" (1 Thess. 5:23). God, having placed the Spirit in us and written God's laws on our hearts and minds, is at work to make us more and more like Christ in our thoughts and actions. Accordingly, the apostle Paul says of himself and the intended recipients of his letter to Rome: "I myself feel confident about you, my brothers and sisters, that you yourselves are full of goodness, filled with all knowledge, and able to instruct one another. Nevertheless on some points I have written to you rather boldly by way of reminder, because of the grace given me by God

to be a minister of Christ Jesus to the Gentiles in the priestly service of the gospel of God, so that the offering of the Gentiles may
be acceptable, sanctified by the Holy Spirit" (Rom. 15:14–16).

Third, we need to enlist our energy in cooperating with God's
process. Again, not motivated by a need to justify ourselves
before God, but living out the justification that is bestowed upon
us by God, we are called to actualize and appropriate what God
is doing in the transforming process.

Frequently, the New Testament scriptures give very direct
commands to perform one kind of behavior or another. Love your
enemy. Share what you own. Do not be conceited. If your enemy
is hungry, feed him. Allow not a hint of immorality among you,
nor any impurity, greed, or drunkenness. They even go so far as
to say, "Be imitators of God" (Eph. 5:1). In giving such commands, the writers, such as Paul, are not holding a dreaded threat
over our heads, "If you don't live perfectly, God will happily
damn you to hell." No. Rather, they are presuming that the power
of Holy Spirit within us will empower us to do what is right.

Consider the promise the apostle gives us: "No testing has
overtaken you that is not common to everyone. God is faithful,
and he will not let you be tested beyond your strength, but with
the testing he will also provide the way out so that you may be
able to endure it" (1 Cor. 10:13). If God is seeing to it that we not
enter into temptation beyond our capacity to resist, and if God is
within us to build Christ's character into us, then all that remains
is for us to follow the lead of the indwelling Spirit. "Live by the
Spirit and you will not gratify the desires of the sinful nature,"
Paul says (Gal. 5:16 NIV).

A former pastor of mine, Malcolm Smith, offers this analogy.
If I were to tell you that steel can fly, you'd laugh at me. You'd say,
"Don't be silly." But if I were to tell you with a serious expression on my face that a huge piece of steel could fly, you'd argue
that the laws of gravity would pull it right down to the ground.
But if I still insisted, saying that a really huge piece of steel could
fly, and it could also take a few hundred people along with it, you
would realize that I am right. A Boeing 747 jet, made with tons
of steel, does that very thing. Why can it fly? Because the laws of
aerodynamics overcome the law of gravity.

When we live by a higher law, the lower law does not cease to exist, but we elevate to the higher. We all are affected by the laws of our own nature that pull us down, but the apostle tells us, "For the law of the Spirit of life in Christ Jesus has set you free from the law of sin and of death" (Rom. 8:2). A higher law has lifted us, elevated us, animated us, and we can live in that law.

We do so supernaturally, living by the Spirit, in the Spirit, and from the Spirit. Because we live by the Spirit, let us keep in step with the Spirit. Each of us has experienced the feeling of standing on a parent's shoes and holding on as he or she walks us around. Any teenager knows what it is like to walk right behind another teen, kicking the leader's shoes as they go. We watch in amazement as Ginger Rogers and Fred Astaire match step for step all around a dance floor. In either case the picture produced is that of keeping in step with the leader. That is what we are to do to live the presence of the Spirit—keep in step as the Spirit leads.

The interface between God's activity and ours may be illustrated each time we take a quarter out of our change purses. Look on the one side of the quarter and you will find the profile of the person, namely, America's first president, George Washington. Flip over the coin and you will see the exalted bald eagle. The one side points to our humanity, our feet firmly planted on the ground. The other side sends us soaring, carried aloft on eagle's wings. Every thought, every action we take incorporates both sides of the coin. They involve both our very human decision and God's courage and fortitude as empowered by Holy Spirit at work within us.

Paul expressed this interface when writing to the Christians in Philippi: "Therefore, my beloved, just as you have always obeyed me, not only in my presence, but much more now in my absence, work out your own salvation with fear and trembling; for it is God who is at work in you, enabling you both to will and to work for his good pleasure" (Phil. 2:12–13). Extend yourself in living forth your new relationship in Christ, he says, all the while remembering that God is working in you to bring it about.

The Bible holds forth no illusions about our humanity. Perfection will never be attained in this life. Accordingly, the most spiritual of Christians make a habit of confessing their failures and sins to God to again be forgiven. We never cease to be sinners. But by God's grace, Christ's sacrificial death, and the infilling of the Spirit, we are accorded the status of sainthood. It remains for us to become in practice what he says we are. Becoming who we are is the sum challenge of living the presence of the Spirit, that is: becoming the holiness of God in action as well as status; becoming the power of God in service as well as intent; becoming the proclaimers of the gospel in interpersonal witness as well as in private prayers; becoming the back on which God bears the world's burdens, the hands through which God touches, the mouthpiece through which God speaks, the arms by which God comforts—becoming who we are.

One important twist needs our attention—that little pronoun *we*. When Holy Spirit was given that Pentecost day, Holy Spirit was given not merely to individuals but to a company of people. Although each had his or her tongue of fire, all shared the sound of the mighty wind. And when the apostle Peter finished preaching and when three thousand embraced the gospel message, they were not merely saved by grace through faith; they were also "added to their number" (Acts 2:41, 47). The privilege of being the dwelling of the Spirit was as much a group privilege as an individual one.

Let us turn our attention to the shared experience of living the presence of the Spirit.

13

Which Is Thy Body?

Some years ago I heard my pastor frequently categorize two kinds of Christians, true Christians and nominal Christians, the latter being those who go to church and the former being those who have accepted Jesus as their Lord and Savior. True Christians, it was said accurately, have entered into a personal relationship with Jesus Christ; they have been converted from a life lived for themselves into a life lived for God. Nominal Christians, on the other hand, were those who go to church week after week but evidence no real personal relationship with Jesus as Savior.

Today a new nominalism has crept into American Christianity. Now that public life does not demand that people attend church to get a good job or to make friends, the number of worshipers lacking a relationship with Jesus is shrinking. However, an exponentially growing number of people say they have accepted Christ, but they don't darken a church door for weeks—even years. They say: "I know the Lord. I'm going to heaven. I just don't have time for church"; or, "I had a falling out with the pastor in my last church, so I just read the Bible and pray on my own."

Such comments and patterns point up a horrendous confusion about living the Christian life, the Spirit-filled life. To accept Christ is to be added to Christ's church. The New Testament Christians knew no substitute for living in Christian communities.

The practical reasons for affiliating as Christians are obvious: mutual support in crisis, continual help in learning God's word and will, combining of resources for missions, corporate expression of worship, and prayer to God. The spiritual reasons for coming together may not be as obvious.

When the apostle Paul was dealing with difficulties among the Christians in Corinth, he had to confront a pervasive wickedness: wretched immorality in individuals' lives and corrosive conflict in the congregation's community life. He addressed them by appealing to the Corinthians' understanding of God's presence in and among them.

In keeping with the movement of God's presence—from the garden to the mountain to the tabernacle to the temple to the incarnate Immanuel—the apostle Paul takes up the same language to speak of the Presence-Spirit.

Regarding personal immorality, he wrote: "Shun fornication! Every sin that a person commits is outside the body; but the fornicator sins against the body itself. Or do you not know that your body is a temple of the Holy Spirit within you, which you have from God, and that you are not your own? For you were bought with a price; therefore glorify God in your body" (1 Cor. 6:18–20). Note the equating of our human bodies with the biblical Temple. What was the purpose of the Temple? The Temple served as a dwelling place for God, who dwelt there by way of Holy Spirit-Presence. Now God lives not in temples made of cloth or stone, but in temples God created—human hearts. In fact, the Greek word used by the apostle, translated *temple,* is the word that was used specifically for the Holy of Holies in the core of the Temple.

Each one of you, Paul says, is a Holy of Holies. Therefore, by no means should you ever subject that temple to sins of sexual immorality. That would be like turning the Holy of Holies into a whorehouse. Now that is a horrible thought! No doubt, Paul made his point to the Corinthians.

On the other hand, the Corinthians had just as difficult a time dealing with their sins against one another. These sins were somewhat less scandalous. They would not create national headlines or be featured on tabloid TV programs, but they were evil nevertheless.

The Corinthian church was a divided congregation. The lines of demarcation between factions are hard for us to trace, because they were drawn every which way and often overlapped. One set of lines was drawn by leader-loyalists. Some Corinthians followed intently the emphases taught by the apostle Peter, whereas others were loyal to Apollos or Paul. Still others, claiming to be more spiritual, stuck just to Jesus. They argued on behalf of their hero and snubbed the teaching of the others God had sent to witness God's word to them.

Another set of lines was drawn over the experience of the miraculous. Some had received the gift of speaking in tongues, not unlike what was received on Pentecost. They claimed that unless a person spoke in tongues, he or she must not really have the Spirit and hence could not truly be a Christian. The others defended themselves but were generally drowned out by the cacophony of spiritual braggarts.

Yet another set of lines was drawn over the use of kosher foods and other related Jewish traditions. Some maintained the strict guidelines, bragging of their rightness before God. Others disregarded such traditions, bragging of their freedom in Christ.

Still another set of lines was drawn over economics. The church had members who sported great wealth—many of whom believed their prosperity to be God's endorsement of their goodness. But the church had many poor, even indentured slaves, who felt scorn toward the rich landowners who would greet them warmly in church but would overwork them on the job while grudgingly paying them beggar's wages.

In the same letter, the apostle takes up the same imagery to address their divisions. About the collective congregation, he asks: "Do you not know that you [all] are God's temple and that God's Spirit dwells in you [all]? If anyone destroys God's temple, God will destroy that person. For God's temple is holy, and you [all] are that temple" (1 Cor. 3:16–17). Lest you miss the subtleties, each use of the word "you" in those verses is explicitly a plural pronoun, whereas the word "temple" is a singular noun. In other words, the people together comprise the one temple of God, and absolutely no one must cause that temple to fragment.

How striking! Again the term for Holy of Holies is used, now with the news that the people together comprise the dwelling place of God. This echoes the words of Jesus: "For where two or three are gathered in my name, I am there among them" (Matt. 18:20).

This identification of the church is reinforced in Paul's second letter to the Corinthians wherein he writes, "For we are the temple of the living God; as God said, 'I will live in them and walk among them, and I will be their God, and they shall be my people'" (2 Cor. 6:16).

As the collective temple, the church automatically includes all Christians. By entry into the church we find the faith to believe, and, correspondingly, faith provides the basis for our entry. Our union with other believers makes possible the knitting of the sons and daughters of God into a community of support and solidarity that protects our solitude from falling into isolation.

Back when Holy Spirit was poured out upon the company of 120 and then received almost immediately by three thousand others, what did they do? They began meeting together in each other's homes, eating together, learning together, praying together, even paying bills together. Yes, they shared what they had with those who had not. Amazingly, there is no hint in the biblical record that such openhandedness was legislated. Rather, it seems that the generosity was a spontaneous outpouring of love and gratitude because of the experience of this new reality— being the temple of the Spirit.

But those Corinthians really blundered. Unfortunately, the one time when they should have noticed how discombobulated their divisions had become was when the factions became most stark—in the sharing of the Lord's Supper.

This Is My Body

Consider for a moment the significance of meals—no, not the food, but the company with whom you eat the food.

Jesus got into trouble for his choice of tablemates. His accusers did not like the company he kept. When they articulated their accusations, they said that he ate with sinners and publicans—not simply that he spent time with them, but that he *ate* with them.

When teenagers start a new school year, one of the most pressing and traumatizing decisions they have to make is where to sit in the cafeteria. They don't want to be seen with the wrong crowd; don't want to sit alone; don't want to sit with people who won't talk to them; don't want to sit with people they don't know. The "don't want to's" go on and on. If you think about it, where did the civil rights movement of the 1960s begin? In luncheonettes! There for the first time African Americans had the nerve to sidle up next to European Americans. The rest is history.

In the early church, the work of the Spirit was largely being celebrated over supper fellowships. Yet in Corinth, the cracks of divisions were surfacing. The believers continued the Jerusalem tradition of gathering on the Lord's Day for worship and dinner. They also continued the tradition of the mother church, with each person expected to bring some food so all could share from the accumulated bounty.

In the year A.D. 51, the fissures in the Corinthian church blew sky high, yet many did not notice. In the years of A.D. 48 and 49, a devastating drought in Italy had wiped out the summer's wheat crops. In A.D. 50 the crops rebounded a bit, but in A.D. 51 they were almost entirely destroyed. The emperor announced that Rome would pay whatever it would take to get grain with which to feed the citizens. Over a thousand miles to the east, such grain could be bought in the region of Asia Minor, where today sits the nation of Turkey. So the emperor sent ships there to buy and transport grain back to Rome. In order to get there, the ships had to get past Greece. They could sail south around Greece's Peloponnesos, but the waters there were treacherous; ships capsized often, never to be heard from again. Instead, the ships were taken to the middle of Greece's west coast, where this generally wide peninsula narrowed to an isthmus, the Isthmus of Corinth. Shipments could be carried over the short stretch of land dividing the west port from the east and, when loaded onto a second ship, could be on their way to Rome.

Of course, the shipowners were happy to sell some of their grain to the Corinthians, just as long as they were willing to pay the same premium prices paid by the emperor.

The Corinthians enjoyed their much-valued grain, but the effects of inflation stung. The wealthy complained incessantly about the prices. The poor went without. Soon the poor members were showing up late to worship, for they had to work seven days a week. They were bringing less and less food with them. Impatient for the poor to arrive and not willing to perpetuate the inequity, the wealthy decided that the Lord's Day agapé feast ("love feast," as it had been called) should no longer be a potluck smorgasbord meal but a "bring your own" meal. Everyone, they contended, should be able to eat his or her own cooking and not have to wait for the tardy arrivers.

The wealthy hardly noticed when some of the poorer members came emptyhanded. Few noticed as some grew gaunt and unusually thin. When some took sick, the others kept their distance lest they be infected. When a few died, the deaths were attributed to other causes, like poor hygiene or the judgment of God. Nobody considered the possibility that some fellow church members were actually dying of malnutrition.

Paul was incensed. "Now in the following instructions I do not commend you," he wrote, "because when you come together it is not for the better but for the worse" (1 Cor. 11:17).

Paul then expounded his rebuke: how they used the gathering to try to show off God's approval of them; how many were eating before others gathered; how some were even getting drunk; how the whole exercise was bringing humiliation to those who had to go without. He then reiterated the words Jesus had uttered prior to serving the Last Supper: "This is my body. . . . This cup is the new covenant in my blood" (vs. 24–25). He expressed then the gravity of such a meal and the possibility of bringing judgment and disfavor on oneself for not eating properly.

Then Paul wove a brilliant play on words. It hinged on his use of the word *body*. People often speak of the church as the body of Christ. That originates in the teachings of Paul, who said that we together are the body through which Christ is at work, with the Lord being the head of that body. Here, while commenting on the Lord's Supper, he says, "Examine yourselves, and only then eat of the bread and drink of the cup. For all who eat and drink without discerning the body, eat and drink judgment against themselves" (vs. 28–29).

Paul then returns to the basic concern: "For this reason many of you are weak and ill, and some have died. . . . So then, my brothers and sisters, when you come together to eat, wait for one another" (vs. 30–33).

Which body is Paul speaking of—the body of Jesus represented in the bread or the body of Christ expressed through the church? The answer is "Both." Having introduced the problem of relationships in the church, he then focused attention on our relationship with Christ in communion but then returned to his original point—now having demonstrated the organic unity between our relationship to God and our relationship to the church community.

To use John's words: "Those who say, 'I love God,' and hate their brothers or sisters, are liars; for those who do not love a brother or sister whom they have seen, cannot love God whom they have not seen. The commandment we have from him is this: those who love God must love their brothers and sisters also" (1 John 4:20–21).

The upward gaze that is naturally evoked in communion, says Paul, needs to evoke an outward gaze. We recognize the body of Christ when we look around at one another and check to see if we are effectively caring for one another. What's more, the outward gaze is not a grievous thing but a celebrative thing. Just as birthdays are much more fun to celebrate with a crowd than alone, so too the Lord's presence is much more to be celebrated in the company of God's people. Growing in relationships with them enhances our relationship with him—albeit through some sandpapery personalities that help smooth our rough edges.

To be the temple of Holy Spirit is to be a living fulfillment of the prophets' dream—the presence of God taking up residence in our individual lives and in our community life—all at once and at the same time!

So then, how is it that we can live the presence of the Spirit when the Spirit seems miles away? What IS the rest of the story?

The Whole of the Story

*T*rouble is often incited by overreacting. If you leave your putt three feet short on the first three greens, chances are that on the fourth green you will send your putt five feet beyond the hole. If you resent the poverty in which you were raised, chances are good that you will spoil your children. If your car's alignment keeps pulling to the right, chances are ripe for oversteering to the left. Overreacting often creates more problems than it solves.

Theologians are notorious overreactors. When Martin Luther discovered the message of "justification by grace through faith," he declared that the book of James, with its theme of "faith without works is dead," ought to be extracted from the Bible. When scientists raised questions that doubted the possibility of miracles, biblical scholars soon were de-mythologizing all biblical accounts of miracles. As feminists have sensitized the church to its historic devaluing of women, some scholars have extracted every hint of masculinity from any identification of God—even creating feminine names and identities for "goddesses."

More pertinent to the subject of our study, when Christians rediscover the person and power of Holy Spirit, they can get so enthralled with the palpable experience of God's presence—and so insistent that others share such an experience—that they talk of nothing else. The "old, old story" is neglected in favor of the new.

A thrilling encounter of Holy Spirit can ignite an explosion of enthusiasm and empowerment. For some, however, the experience of the Presence leads to an irrational single-mindedness that brings its own problems. Indeed, through the centuries teachings and experiences of Holy Spirit have turned into unintended Trojan horses.

Late in the second century, one community of faith sought to renew the focus on the experience of Holy Spirit. Gathered together by Montanus in the Asian city of Phrygia, they started out well, even drawing into their fellowship the leading theologian of their day, namely, Tertullian. They passionately stirred up the gift of prophecy, which largely had faded from the church's activity. There was one problem, however: they did not test their prophecies against the words of scripture. Before long they were prophesying Christ's imminent return to their city, which their prophets were now calling the "True Jerusalem." The other branches of the church followed with words of condemnation. Although the movement continued for a few centuries, it was relegated to fringe status.

Throughout the Middle Ages, during the Reformation, during the great awakenings of American history, throughout the twentieth century, movement upon movement has elevated the person and work of Holy Spirit, only to neglect the faithful proclamation of the gospel. In the process, the mainstream church repeatedly has shunned not only the teachings and practices of their fanatical neighbors but also all talk regarding Holy Spirit. Although God certainly was present with God's people, many of them lived as if the Spirit were miles away. Overreacting causes such things to happen.

Is there any chance we can experience Holy Spirit without trifling with—or diminishing the value of—the many other biblical teachings that complete God's self-revelation in scripture? Can we ever hope to comprehend our Christian beliefs in a way that makes intellectual sense while allowing room for the intuitive and emotional? Can our carefully systematized belief structures welcome experiential "in-Spirited" serendipities? Can we march back and forth between Bethlehem's stable, Galilee's fishing boats, Calvary's cross, the garden's empty tomb, and the upper room's prayer circle—and be at home in each of those places? Can our teaching on Holy Spirit help congeal the whole faith for us?

Yes! The answer is "YES!" The whole faith for whole persons in the whole community of faith can be comprehended comprehensively—and simply.

Amazingly, one verse of scripture summarizes the whole faith. One single verse states everything that we need to know about the whole of the biblical story. The verse is quite familiar, quoted in so many churches every Sunday, quoted in many prayers—at least by clergy. For this pastor-writer, I quote it more frequently than any other passage of scripture. But, as in so many other cases, familiarity produces neglect.

No, the verse is not John 3:16, "The gospel in a nutshell" ("For God so loved the world that he gave his only Son, so that everyone who believes in him may not perish but may have eternal life"). The verse is not the Lord's Prayer or one of the Ten Commandments or a beatitude or even the Golden Rule. It is the closing verse of Paul's second letter to the Corinthians, and it is sounded in many worship services as the benediction. How does it read? "The grace of the Lord Jesus Christ, the love of God, and the communion of the Holy Spirit be with all of you."

Truly Trinitarian

This simple verse of scripture summarizes the essence of biblical faith. It portrays the heart of God's identity, character, and mission. It proclaims the good news succinctly and completely. This verse tells what we need to know about the trinitarian God.

Of course, there's just one problem with the Christian doctrine of the Trinity. The word *trinity* does not appear anywhere in scripture. In fact, the exact formula "Father, Son, and Holy Spirit" never appears in scripture in so many words. Nevertheless, the doctrine of the Trinity is one of the cardinal doctrines of all Roman Catholic, Orthodox, and Protestant Christians. It is one of the few universally affirmed Christian beliefs. So many passages in scripture and the overall message of the New Testament make sense only if the doctrine of the Trinity is affirmed at the core of faith. Providentially, the early church leaders saw the way clear to articulate this core belief, and the councils at Nicaea, Chalcedon, and others, formulated the doctrine for the ages. In

spite of centuries of debate and theological reactions and overre-
actions, the biblical doctrine of the Trinity continues to focalize
the core of Christian faith. As recently as 1991, the Presbyterian
Church (U.S.A.) has formulated its beliefs in *A Brief Statement
of Faith,* which outlines the faith around the benediction's trinitarian structure.

Unfortunately, many Christians are not truly trinitarian. They
may recite the Apostles' Creed or the Nicene Creed, but in practice they are really unitarians or binitarians at best. They focus
their whole faith on one member—or at most two members—of
the Trinity.

Many Christians focus their attention solely on Christ. It is
easy to do so, given how visible and tangible Jesus is. Ironically,
Christocentrism is the hallmark of both traditional liberal Christian movements and traditional conservative Christian movements. To the liberal Christian, Jesus is the ultimate role model
for all ethical decision making. The mantra of the liberal movement is "What would Jesus do?" How would Jesus, the champion
of mercy and generosity, act in this circumstance? To the conservative Christian, Jesus is the Savior who died on the cross in
order to redeem sinners for God. The mantra of the conservative
movement rightly could be "What did Jesus do?" What has Jesus
accomplished in his incarnation, crucifixion, and resurrection?
Seen this way, we can see that both movements convey essential
truths. But both, even when taken together, stand incomplete
apart from the rest of the Trinity.

Theocentric Christians focus their attention on God. Some
focus on God in a more intentionally vague way so as to avoid
hints of exclusivity—especially when motivated by the desire to
tear down walls between Christians and believers of other faiths.
Some theocentric Christians focus their attention specifically on
God as Father, especially as a reaction to the feminist movement.
In either case, the resulting theology lacks the whole picture
painted by the Trinity.

Pneumatic Christians focus their attention on Holy Spirit.
Most obviously, Pentecostal and charismatic Christians empha-
size the Spirit because of their highly charged experience of
God's presence and power. On the other hand, radical movements

emphasize the Spirit as the inspirer of ideas they have not learned in the scriptures, but which can be justified by taking out of context those words "The letter kills but the Spirit gives life." Still, both kinds of emphasis upon the Spirit lack the complete picture that is drawn by the Trinity.

Where can we find the complete picture? It is right there in the benediction.

"The Grace of the Lord Jesus Christ, . . .

No word better summarizes the ministry and work of Jesus than does the word *grace*. That is not to say that Jesus spoke of grace per se; in fact, nowhere in the New Testament is he quoted using that word. But his role modeling, his preaching, his parables, his death, and his resurrection all convey a message that the apostles summarized with the simple word *grace*.

Grace is proclaimed in the story of the Good Samaritan, where a dying crime victim is showered with blessings unearned, bestowed by the sheer generosity of a stranger. Grace prevails in the parable of the prodigal son, who, having squandered all his inherited wealth, asks out of his despair to be treated as the lowest of slaves, only to find himself the guest of honor at a family banquet feast. Grace bursts forth in story after story that Jesus told.

Grace is enacted in many of Jesus' encounters with the women, men, and children of his day. When the woman caught in adultery is facing the legal punishment of stoning, Jesus stands in the breech, freeing her from her condemnation and pointing her to a better way to live. As others tried to shoo away the distracting children (the prevailing tradition of that day was that children ought not be seen or heard), Jesus embraced them in love. Although those stricken with leprosy were ostracized for medical reasons and tax collectors were shunned for their complicity in helping Rome oppress the people of God, Jesus touched them, healed them, and broke bread with them. And although honorable men did not speak with women in public and honorable Jews did not speak with godforsaken Samaritans, Jesus held a redemptive conversation with an illicit Samaritan woman at the central gathering place. She, in turn, brought scores of others to meet the Savior.

Jesus lived grace. Jesus also came to extend grace. He launched his preaching ministry by quoting the prophet Isaiah:

"The Spirit of the Lord is upon me,
   because he has anointed me
      to bring good news to the poor.
He has sent me to proclaim release to the captives
   and recovery of sight to the blind,
      to let the oppressed go free,
to proclaim the year of the Lord's favor."
                                    (Luke 4:18–19)

He defended his unholy alliances by declaring, "A physician comes for the sick, not the healthy." He declared that he had come to give others life abundantly. Yes, Jesus died for sinners.

Jesus' whole life, death, resurrection, and ascension are summarized by the word *grace*. Accordingly, years after his ascension, when the apostles were being accused of neglecting the commandments, they wrapped themselves in the flag of Jesus' grace. For example, Peter, defending the Gentile ministry of Paul and Barnabas against the legalists, said, "On the contrary, we believe that we will be saved through the grace of the Lord Jesus, just as they will" (Acts 15:11).

When summarizing the essence of faith, the apostle Paul said, "For by grace you have been saved through faith, and this is not your own doing; it is the gift of God—not the result of works, so that no one may boast" (Eph. 2:8–9).

Indeed, the final verse in all the Bible says, "The grace of the Lord Jesus be with all the saints. Amen" (Rev. 22:21).

So what's so amazing about grace? Grace bestows upon all believers all the benefits of salvation and life-transformation simply because Jesus purchased such benefits for us. Although theologians have formulated intricate explanations of grace, the Sunday school definition says it best: God's Riches at Christ's Expense.

The riches bestowed by God include salvation from sin, redemption from spiritual slavery, adoption as God's children, inclusion into Christ's body, reconciliation with God and one another, sustenance for daily needs, empowerment for significant service, and even more. The expense paid by Christ includes his relinquishment of divine privilege to become a humble human, the struggles of abiding the hate of those opposing him, and enduring the foolishness of those who supported him, the despair of betrayal, the horror of crucifixion—and with it, the experience of banishment when "he who knew no sin became sin for us that we might become the righteousness of God in him"—and the sadness of seeing his dearest loved ones being at a total loss without him.

What is so amazing about grace is that Christ paid such a high price to purchase such a great salvation and that he in turn has given such benefits to you and me simply for the receiving.

That's amazing! What is also amazing is that Christ's grace evokes such great gratitude in those who have received his gifts that they in turn find themselves wanting to be conduits of his grace toward others. Grace received becomes grace conveyed.

Grace is the word that summarizes the work and gift of Christ to all his own.

. . . the Love of God, . . .

The second member of the Trinity mentioned in the benediction is simply God. Through the years, the more specific name, "our Father," has commonly been inserted, in keeping with the many other biblical passages and the creeds that formulate the Trinity as Father, Son, and Holy Spirit. However, when the apostle Paul was writing this letter, he simply spoke of God.

Nevertheless, there is good reason to speak of God as Father. As over against the many other labels in use in that day, Jesus spoke of the almighty as *Abba,* the Aramaic word for Daddy.

The significance of *Abba* is particularly highlighted by noting that the Old Testament calls God father just eight times, whereas the New Testament writers quote Jesus speaking about, or to, God as Father over 250 times. The late gospel scholar J. Arthur Baird insisted that Jesus' central message, even above that of the coming kingdom of God, was that of God as father.

Consider Matthew 6:9—"Pray them in this way: 'Our Father in heaven . . . .'" Consider Matthew 7:11—"If you then, who are evil, know how to give good gifts to your children, how much more will your Father in heaven give good gifts to those who ask him!" Consider Romans 8:15–16—"For you did not receive a spirit of slavery to fall back into fear, but you have received a spirit of adoption. When we cry, 'Abba! Father!' it is that very Spirit bearing witness with our spirit that we are children of God." Consider Galatians 4:6—"And because you are children, God has sent the Spirit of his Son into our hearts, crying, 'Abba! Father!'"

These verses raise a huge difficulty for us today. After centuries of men excluding and even oppressing women, we have been rightly called to redress this injustice. After centuries of women being forced to envision God as a man, many are pleading for feminine images of God. On the more technical level, linguistic scholars and postmodernist deconstructionists have sensitized us to the power of language to give and withhold power from segments of the population. Most obviously, the use of the masculine preference in so many expressions of communication has served the handy purpose of keeping men in the halls of authority and control while keeping the glass ceiling floating above the surface of the women's secretarial pool. In the process, such language use has diminished the quality of men's lives by giving them a distorted, exaggerated sense of their own entitlement and superiority.

The use of language to reinforce the power of masculine privilege and to disempower the feminist majority runs headlong into Jesus' proclamation of God as Father.

How can we speak of God as *Abba,* as Jesus taught? We can't solve all the questions revolving around such a dilemma in this space; a much more thorough and deliberate study is called for than we possibly could engage in these pages. But one essential point can be made: When Jesus spoke of *abba* and prayed to *abba,* his point was not that of genderness but tenderness. The Creator of the world who had revealed God's self to Israel as the almighty, sovereign, transcendent Lord of the universe has been revealed as the shepherd who seeks out lost sheep, as the hen who gathers her chicks under her wing, and as the father who runs to the crest of the hill to welcome the prodigal home.

As Art Baird enlarges: "To know God is not only to know

about God. . . . [T]o really know God in the deepest sense, on God's own terms, is to know God personally, immediately, subjectively; to talk to God in prayer, to commune with God in worship and the secret meditation of the heart, to do God's will in living a life of service to others. . . . GOD IS PERSON and to know God personally is to know God as he is. . . . You can never know God by talking about God. Ultimately, somehow, you have to get down on your knees and talk to God, because God is person."[1]

Accordingly, in the light of such a personhood of God, the benediction penned by Paul speaks simply of "the love of God." That says it.

. . . and the Communion of the Holy Spirit . . ."

The third member of the Trinity, the one who has been the subject of this volume, is Holy Spirit, whose function within the Godhead is summarized by the word *communion.*

Does the word *communion* accurately reflect what we have been sharing about the person and work of Holy Spirit? Does that word crystallize your understanding of the presence of Holy Spirit?

As we have seen, so many believers through the centuries have sought to summarize the role and ministry of Holy Spirit, only to produce meanings that focused on by-products rather than essence. Consider, as an analogy, aliens trying to explain an American pastime. Imagine aliens from another solar system visiting the earth, only to hover just above the view of the fans at a college football game. They return to their own planet and are asked to explain the sport of football. They report, "It is an oblong bowl-shaped stadium, filled with thousands of people cheering and shouting, drinking a substance they call beer and eating pink cylinders held in little cushions and covered with a yellowish paste. They stand up and down in sequence in a thing they call the wave. Then they all go home." If you had heard that

---

1. J. Arthur Baird, *Rediscovering the Power of the Gospels* (Wooster, Ohio: Iona Press, 1982), 45–46.

report, you would protest, "They've missed the point! They haven't said anything about the game on the field."

So it is with Holy Spirit. People keep missing the point. Eccentric religious groups attribute their far-out ideas to the Spirit's inspiration. Demonstrative, emotional outbursts are attributed to the Spirit's elevation. Pentecostals focus on the power of the Spirit. Wesleyans focus on the sanctifying work of the Spirit. Catholics highlight the sacramental means of grace by the Spirit. Reformed bodies attribute the proclamation of the word to the Spirit. Evangelicals count on enablement of evangelism from the Spirit.

But when all is said and done, all those groups are focusing on by-products, not essence. They recognize the natural impact on a human life and on a human community when the almighty, all-holy, all-proclaiming, all-wise, irresistible presence of God shows up in human lives. But such ideas are by-products nonetheless.

What is the essence of the work of Holy Spirit? The apostle Paul says the essence can be found in one word—*koinonia*. *Koinonia* is a Greek word taken from the root *koinos,* which means common, and from the enlarged word *koinoneo* (pronounced "koin-o-neh-o"), meaning to share in common. *Koinonia* itself means partnership, companionship, and fellowship. Does that ring a bell?

Jesus had indeed promised the coming of the Advocate "to be with you forever." He added, "You know him, because he abides with you, and he will be in you" (John 14:16–17).

In the powerful elucidation of essential Christian beliefs found in the book of Romans, the apostle Paul reflects: "God's love has been poured into our hearts through the Holy Spirit that has been given to us" (Rom. 5:5).

The apostle John, reflecting late in life, reminds the faith community: "By this we know that we abide in him [God] and he in us, because he has given us of his Spirit" (1 John 4:13).

The essential role and ministry of Holy Spirit is that of uniting with you, and you in turn to other believers, in order to bring us into partnership, companionship, and fellowship with God.

Put together in the context of the Trinity, one could say that, given that the God of love has yearned from eternity past to adopt us as children, and given that the grace of the Lord Jesus Christ has paid the ultimate price to tear down the veil of sin-weaved separation between humanity and the Godhead, Holy Spirit was poured out upon all those brought by grace to faith. This was done in order to bestow the benefits of Christ's salvation, chiefest of which is simply the presence of God dwelling within each believer and uniting the community of faith.

What is the whole of the story? It is found in the words of the benediction: "The grace of the Lord Jesus Christ, the love of God, and the communion of the Holy Spirit be with all of you."

One further clarification must be added. When sounded, the words of the benediction sometimes come across like a fleeting hope, like "I hope you win the lottery." But is that what the apostle was saying? Was the "grace of the Lord Jesus Christ" something that Paul hoped just might show up in people's lives? By no means! The grace of Christ is the sure ground on which all believers can place their complete confidence! Was the "love of God" a disposition that Paul hoped a capricious deity might choose among many other alternatives? Of course not! God was, is, and always will be the embodiment of love!

So why do we speak of the presence of Holy Spirit as if the Spirit were living on a celestial elevator, showing up at one moment and disappearing the next? Why do we treat the third member of the Trinity as an emotion, an inner consciousness, or merely a magic wand? Why do we place Holy Spirit on the end of a stick to be suspended out in front of us—but never to be attained—like the racehorse experiences the dangling carrot?

It is time to see that Holy Spirit is so much more than our perceptions, so much more than a feeling or a force. Holy Spirit is a person, the very person of God about whom the apostolic faith speaks as abiding in each and every believer inwardly, permanently, reconcilingly, transformingly, emperingly, proclaimingly. The *koinonia* of Holy Spirit is as sure a thing as is the grace of the Lord Jesus Christ and the love of God.

Yes, that is not only the rest of the story; it is the whole of the story. So hear it once again: "The grace of our Lord Jesus Christ, the love of God, and the communion of the Holy Spirit be with all of you."